728

D0716986

Key Buildings of the Twentieth Century

Volume 2: Houses 1945–1989

Dedicated to the memory of Jacob Black-Michaud

Key Buildings of the Twentieth Century

Volume 2: Houses 1945–1989

David Dunster

Butterworth Architecture

London Boston Singapore Sydney Toronto Wellington

Butterworth Architecture
is an imprint of Butterworth-Heinemann Ltd.

PART OF REED INTERNATIONAL P.L.C.

First published 1990

British Library Cataloguing in Publication Data
Dunster, David
    Key buildings of the twentieth century.
    Vol. 2, Houses, 1945–1989
    1. Buildings. Architectural features, 1900–
    I. Title
    724.6

    ISBN 0–408–50029–8

Library of Congress Cataloging-in-Publication Data
(Revised for. vol. 2)

Dunster, David.
    Key buildings of the twentieth century.

    Vol. 2 has imprint: London; Boston: Butterworth
Architecture.
    Includes bibliographical references.
    Contents: v. 1. Houses, 1900–1944 – – v. 2. Houses,
1945–1989.
    1. Architecture, Modern– –20th century.   2. Buildings
– –Designs and plans.   I. Key buildings of the 20th
century.   III. Title.
    NA680.D86   1985   728'.37'0904   85–42945
    ISBN 0–8478–0642–1 (pbk. : vol. 1)
    ISBN 0–408–50029–8 (v. 2)

Photoset by TecSet Ltd, Wallington, Surrey
Printed and bound by Hartnolls Ltd., Bodmin,
Cornwall

Contents

All the drawings have been completely re-drawn from published material. The process of re-drawing was to blow up the published material to a scale of 1:100. The drawings were then all reduced to exactly the same scale, 1:250, which provided the basis for the layout.

Preface 1

1945	Ludwig Mies van der Rohe (1886–1969)	Farnsworth House, Plano, Illinois, USA	6
1947	Luis Barragán (1902–1988)	Own House, Tacubaya, Mexico City	8
1948	Bruce Goff (1904–1982)	Ford House, Aurora, Illinois, USA	12
1948	Richard Neutra (1892–1970)	Warren Tremaine House, Santa Barbara, California, USA	14
1949	Charles Eames (1907–1978)	Eames' House, Pacific Palisades, California, USA	16
1949	Ralph Erskine (b. 1914)	House for Elof Nilsson, Storvik-Hammarby, Sweden	18
1949	Le Corbusier (1887–1965)	House for Dr Curuchet, La Plata, Argentina	20
1951	Frank Lloyd Wright (1867–1959)	Price House, Phoenix, Arizona, USA	22
1953	Alvar Aalto (1898–1976)	Summerhouse, Muuratsalo, Finland	24
1953	Philip Johnson (b. 1906)	Wiley House, New Canaan, Connecticut, USA	26
1953	Oscar Niemeyer (b. 1907)	Own House, Rio de Janeiro, Brazil	28
1953	Jorn Utzon (b. 1918)	House at Hellebæk, Denmark	30
1955	Le Corbusier (1887–1965)	House for Mrs Manorama Sarabhai, Ahmedabad, India	32
1955	Alison (b. 1928) and Peter (b. 1923) Smithson	Sugden House, Watford, UK	34
1956	Jean Prouvé (1901–1984)	Prototype House for L'Abbé Pierre, Nancy, France	36
1956	James Stirling (b. 1926) and James Gowan (b. 1923)	House at Cowes, Isle of Wight, UK	38
1958	Atelier 5	Merz House, Switzerland	40
1958	Oswald Mathias Ungers (b. 1926)	Own House, Mungersdorff, West Germany	44
1959	Edward Cullinan (b. 1931)	Marvin House, Stinson Beach, California, USA	46
1959	Egon Eierman (1904–1970)	Own House, Baden Baden, West Germany	48
1960	John Voelcker (1927–1972)	House at Arkley, Hertfordshire, UK	50
1961	Louis I. Kahn (1901–1974)	Esherick House, Chestnut Hill, Philadelphia, USA	52
1962	Charles Moore (b. 1925)	Own House, Orinda, California, USA	54
1962	Robert Venturi (b. 1925) and John Rauch (b. 1930)	Mother's House, Chestnut Hill, Philadelphia, USA	56
1964	James Gowan (b. 1923)	Schreiber House, London, UK	58
1966	Paul Rudolph (b. 1918)	Town House, New York, USA	62

1966	Team 4 – Richard Rogers (b. 1933), Su Rogers (1940), Wendy Foster (1935–1989), Norman Foster (b. 1935)	House at Creek Vean, Cornwall, UK	64
1966	Team 4 – Richard Rogers (b. 1933), Su Rogers (1940), Wendy Foster (1935–1989), Norman Foster (b. 1935)	Jaffé House, Hertfordshire, UK	66
1967	Michael Graves (b. 1934)	Hanselmann House, Fort Wayne, Indiana, USA	68
1967	John Howard (1930–1968)	Mews House, London, UK	72
1967	Frei Otto (b. 1925) with Rob Krier (b. 1938)	House and Studio at Warmbronn, West Germany	74
1970	Robert Venturi (b. 1925) and John Rauch (b. 1930)	Trubeck and Wislocki Houses, Nantucket, Massachusetts, USA	76
1971	Alvaro Siza do Vieira (b. 1933)	Cardoso House, Modelo do Minho, Portugal	78
1972	Lluis Clotet (b. 1941) and Oscar Tusquets (b. 1941)	Casa Vittoria, Pantelleria, Sicily, Italy	80
1972	Richard Meier (b. 1934)	Shamberg Pavilion, Chappaqua, New York, USA	82
1973	Frank Westergaard	House at Herning, Denmark	84
1974	Rob Krier (b. 1938)	House, Luxembourg	86
1974	Robert A.M. Stern (b. 1939)	Town House, New York, USA	88
1975	William Turnbull	Zimmerman House, Fairfax County, Virginia, USA	90
1976	Peter Eisenman (b. 1932)	House VI, Cornwall, Connecticut, USA	92
1976	Fabio Reinhardt (b. 1942) and Bruno Reichlin (b. 1941)	Casa Tonino, Ticino, Switzerland	94
1977	Taller d'Arquitectura	House at Montras, Spain	96
1978	Tadao Ando (b.1941)	Horiuchi House, Osaka, Japan	98
1978	Frank Gehry (b. 1929)	Own House, Santa Monica, California, USA	100
1978	Marco Zanuso (b. 1930)	House on Lake Como, Italy	102
1979	Andrew Batey (b. 1944) and Mark Mack (b. 1949)	Kirlin House, Napa Valley, California, USA	104
1979	Mario Botta (b. 1943)	House at Ligornetto, Ticino, Switzerland	106
1984	Jeronimo Junquera (b. 1943) and Estanislao Peréz Pita (b. 1943)	House at Santander, Spain	108
1985	Glen Murcutt (b. 1936)	House at Bingie Point, New South Wales, Australia	110
1987	Eldred Evans (b. 1939) and David Shalev (b. 1937)	House at Twickenham, Middlesex, UK	112
1989	Maggie Edmond (b. 1946) and Peter Corrigan (b. 1939)	Athan House, Monbulk, Victoria, Australia	114

Preface

Between 1900 and 1945 modern houses were designed either as prototypes for repetitive housing schemes or as the twentieth-century version of the nineteenth-century bourgeois villa. Few schemes were built in the inter-war period that used the experimental results of the prototypes, and villas depending on live-in servants have tended in the post-1945 period to become the model for institutional buildings such as galleries and museums.

In retrospect the work of that first 45-year period appears heroic, and we know that heroism can take either epic or tragic form. The epic dimensions successfully cut free from the traditions of nineteenth-century architectural practice. (Architectural theorists from that century have fared better than its architects.) The severance was not simply negative, meaning a determined cutting out of ornament, pastiche or stylism. The boldness of gesture and intensity of expression would have been immaterial without the mood of optimism and idealism experienced after the traumas of World War I. Removing the traces of the past was thus a new beginning, part of the necessary process of rebirth which could both dismiss the past and look forward to a new future.

Questions such as what could twentieth-century architecture look like, with what could it concern itself – the form of cities, of landscapes and of Society – these questions could only be raised in an atmosphere of confidence and optimism, even if that might approach messianic euphoria. The epic of pre-World War II architecture is the odyssey which returned practice to the harbour of architecture after the confusion of the labyrinthine journey through the nineteenth century. The tragedy, aside from the colossal number of unbuilt projects, has been, since 1945, a struggle against the degeneration of that epic optimism, for reasons which are mostly outside the immediate field of architecture. There is more than one aspect of comedy, however, and that has been the impulse to form a modern vernacular. The houses selected for illustration here are some indication of the dimensions of that struggle.

In my introduction to Volume 1, I argued, following Philip Johnson, that there was no such thing as a post-modern plan. Four years later nothing has been designed that would change my mind. What has become clearer in compiling this volume has been how sophisticated were the architects of this post-World War II period with respect to history.

I would like to argue that this sophistication is the distinguishing mark of these works. The history of architecture registers in two ways: the first is a general consciousness of the tradition and masterworks of European architecture. The second register is critical, often virulently antagonistic to the more immediate works of this century. The first register is available because of the pioneering histories developed by those twentieth-century historians who finally established architectural history as a specialized branch of the history of art. Not only in books, but also in lectures delivered with proselytizing zeal by such as Colin Rowe, Reyner Banham, Bruno Zevi, and above all Vincent Scully. These men depended on historians of the stature of Pevsner, Giedion, Wittkower, Hitchcock and Blunt, each more cautiously enthusiastic than their students, mindful perhaps of the struggles they experienced to establish the discipline of architectural history.

The history of European architecture became then a field of academic endeavour always subject to more intense research but based upon a canon of buildings which could be visited. Even if cracked and leaking from lack of upkeep, they, the villas of Palladio for example, existed as a testament to a history of architectural thought. The idea was more powerful than the fabric, and often the fabric was a hulk hundreds of years on. But the plan could be drawn, the diagram remembered. If the history of European architecture comprised work, some of which was in ruins, what was left held enough to support criticism and analysis.

Architects of this period, faced with the fragments of an architectural past, reconstructed the buildings as objects in their minds through the abstraction of the plan. That effort alone would have been enough to generate a more intellectual, generalized view of history. In turn it produced a suite of theoretical gestures whose task was to rebuild the bridge to the traditions of pre-twentieth-century architecture which the epoch-making predecessors had had to destroy. The rejection was polemical in order for them to feel themselves capable and confident enough to make architecture anew. All of those 'pioneers' had been educated within a historically valued tradition of great works from the past. The ease with whey they argued against its continuation arose from self-reflection, the essential characteristic of Modernism in all the arts. This reflex therefore provides the basis for the second register of history – that which by treating history as a sequence of stylistic episodes lays bare the possibility of choosing one predecessor over any other.

But the second and later generations could not position themselves with such a simple wave of the hand. While they could make diagrams of the buildings of the past, their immediate forefathers presented a paradox. Was it necessary to kill those people who had founded the Modernist movement in architecture, as the previous generation had rejected the practitioners of architectural tradition? The inescapable paradox of this question led in the post-war period to a great diversity of forms and approaches, as each new young architect had to interpret the history of Modernism for himself or herself.

The simple rules of logical positivism offered a way out, leading to the over-evaluation of pragmatics in the idea of the 'lore of the operation', which inexorably leads to the idea of 'the style for the job'. In both formulas, historical references could enter through the back door. When Saarinen's Styles and Morse College at Yale was opened, his debt to San Gimigniano was openly acknowledged and openly arbitrary. Where would there be any economy in the use of history? What logic could govern borrowing?

In tandem the human sciences, having already in the inter-war period investigated the kinds of history which could be conceived of, began to re-evaluate the roles of myth within societies. Firstly through anthropology the idea of 'primitive', 'savage' or 'uncivilised' succumbed before an onslaught of research. All races, all peoples seemed, in the eyes of the structuralists, to be equally 'advanced' and certainly exhibited similar organizational patterns of behaviour and thought. Mythic thought was rehabilitated. If 'the house' as a term is too Platonic, too essentialist and too metaphysical, none the less as a term it could now be employed because anthropology taught both the ubiquitousness of the purpose, and the universality of rituals to do with the Building of the House, which even for Beethoven who wrote an overture called 'The Consecration of the House' still carried mystical power.

The net result of this particular development in the human sciences was the rejection of the verbal material of Modernism. If my example is drawn from anthropology, equally valid demonstrations could be drawn from the valorization of popular culture undertaken by Roland Barthes, not uncritically, and by Marshall MacLuhan, with considerably more sympathy. In language itself words were tainted; the 500 words of plain English themselves presented a view of the world, held by a minority. The vernacular itself in speech or architecture could be argued to be not innocent but instead guilty of subordinating both freedom and desire.

Architects, never the most avid readers, had, by some intuition, arrived at comparable intuitions contemporary to the discoveries of the human sciences.

The Modern Movement, as a canonized entity, could have approached the house as a spiritual manifestation, through Ruskin, Bergson or Hegel. And there existed a desired *rapprochement* between mass culture and architecture through the logistics of serial production, Fordism, Taylorism, the God Efficiency or simply mass-production. But the mythic understanding of Lévi Strauss is in no way a manifestation of human spirituality but instead an attempt to demonstrate the deep structure inside the human mind. The vernacular, a theme dependent on an architecture of place, local materials and traditions is almost a bastion against the evils of mass-production – specifically the suburban sprawl. Its rationale has little to do with efficiency, management or serial repetition. Indeed vernacular things are sophisticated, allowing a restricted individuality within a common, albeit local order.

This is not simply a roundabout route to justify the use of bricks. The changed arguments indicate changes of consciousness and value exposed at the verbal level by the human sciences and manifested in the arts by parallel but different phenomena. To some extent the notion of a *zeitgeist* cannot be resisted, save for the impossibility of following the Hegelian or Burckhardtian track of searching for one single sole idea that a dialectic between form and thought might manifest. The researches of Venturi, Rossi, Ungers and Stirling and Gowan, to name only the most famous, are unthinkable without the changed economic–political but above all philosophical climate in which those researches were undertaken.

To call them researchers, these architects, is perhaps disturbing. But if we fail to recognize that ideas are in play then all that is left within any theoretical description of architecture is a Tafurian play of action–reaction, of the stylistic equivalent of short skirts being immediately followed by long skirts, inevitably leading to a market place of style. The house as a mythic container for domestic familial ritual, the notion of a vernacular of Modernism sufficiently flexible to be both current and traditional, these two ideas are the epicentres of the work illustrated here. At one level of perception the unities of approach are boring, too similar to demonstrate any serious development from the early renaissance of the twenties. Mannerist architecture is of course very much a category invented and promoted in the 1950s. It describes a sixteenth-century period between Alberti, Brunelleschi and Michelangelo. If the Baroque is included that makes the period one that lasts nearly 200 years. The changes brought about by the experiments of the twenties established a framework within which the work of the post-war period is firmly based.

An analogy with the development from the art of the Early Renaissance to that of Mannerism and the Baroque is instructive. The basis of geometrical setting out by quadrature combined with a rebirth of 'civilisation' seen by Northern Italians to refer to a Graeco–Roman ideal, can easily be equated to the interest of Modernism in columnar grids. The grid represents a universe of equal points, and a universal possibility applicable everywhere. Instead of the return to a Graeco–Roman ideal, the Modernist grid copies some notion of progress through knowledge available to all members of society.

The analogy works better as a structuralist one than in specific detail. The concept of civilisation to which Alberti addressed himself is wider than the narrow professional limits of architecture with which the first Moderns concerned themselves. Herein lies a weakness that gave the occasion for the work in mythic exploration and vernacular assemblage. If the new architecture of the twenties was *a fortiori* a mechanism by which the audience of clients could lead a twentieth-century life, that mechanism reduced the potentials for living to a strict code of tidiness, an aesthetic of almost Zen-like objectness. Familiar things in that architecture were de-familiarized by the space between them, literally by the disposition of paintings, carpets and objects about the internal spaces as if those spaces were part of an exhibition. Everyday clutter was too Victorian.

This effect denied the acquisitive tendencies of the new bourgeoisie and of the emerging sophistication of a proletariat. Since 1945, the design of houses has had to accept a more varied, denser domestic interior than is conceivable in the Villa Savoye, or the Farnsworth pavilion. The bookcase and cabinet may become built-in shelving but only in magazines are objects arranged thereon with the delicacy of a curator. 'No possessions' equals poverty. The minimalist aesthetic contradicts the acquisitive society.

The architectural effects on post-war housing have thus been to permit a greater variety of forms, plans, sections than could have been acceptable to architects before. To some this is to return to a more nineteenth-century interior. These directions are not illustrated here, because that work is already historically known. But where compositional techniques such as collage, montage, collision and fragmentation have been employed then the processes of Modernism are maintained. Even if borrowed from other parts, these processes are inimical to Modernism which to a greater degree is concerned with the authenticity of process than with any aesthetic of product. Collage, montage, collision and fragmentation depend on pre-existing ideas and objects. But the juxtapositions place the pre-existing in a new light and change its nature. When Venturi 'collides' a staircase and a fireplace in a bath of north-easterly light he borrows ideas from Wright in the collision and Le Corbusier in the spatial experience. Thereby he can reunite motifs which have degenerated too much and recall a sense of newness in an original proposition that works with both a history and a myth. The history is that of twentieth-century housing, the myth is that the hearth and staircase are the centre of any house. The process by which he brings this off relies more heavily upon the concepts of literary work, the exegesis of the New Criticism, which in turn depend upon a notion that any work of art can be understood best if thought about in its own terms. The process looks for autonomous generative rules rather than codes or laws that depend upon a canon, a tradition or a history. Genres will be mixed.

   These arguments are small clues to an obviously heterogeneous selection. No unifying manifesto underpins the superstructure of the variety of houses I selected. Mao's injunction to allow a thousand ideas to blossom and contend is still the best excuse for stylistic pluralism I know. The emphasis ought to be on 'contend'. Since 1945 we have seen already four generations of students pass through architectural training. This book is dedicated to my great friend Jacob Black-Michaud who loved architecture. He would have accepted the hope that a memorial is nothing beside the objective of open knowledge.

David Dunster
London, April 1989

PHOTOGRAPHIC CREDITS

Page

7	Howard Dearstyne's Estate
11	Luis Barragán
13	Architectural Association Slide library/S. Mintz
17	Architectural Association Slide library/J. Stirling
21	Alan Morris
25	Steven Groak
27	Architectural Association Slide library/D. Jackson
29	Architectural Association Slide library/P. Cook
31	K. Helmer-Petersen
35	Roger Hillier (left); Simon Dell (right)
39	James Gowan
40–42	Atelier 5/Albert Winkler
45	Architectural Association Slide library/J. Bogle
47	Edward Cullinan
51	H. Lyttleton
70–71	Michael Graves/Jim Offerle
73	John Kaine
83	Architectural Association Slide library/A. Minchin
87	Rob Krier
89	E. Stoeklein
91	William Turnbull
93	Peter Eisenman
95	Werner KRHS
99	The Japan Architect/Mitsuo Matsuoka (left); Tadao Ando (right)
101	Architectural Association Slide library/H. Cook
105	Reiner Blunck (left); Tim Street-Porter (right)
110–111	Max Dupain
115	Edmond/Corrigan

Ludwig Mies van der Rohe: Farnsworth House

1945

The site is a flood plain of a river glimpsed through the copse. The house that Mies erected is a steel frame, totally glazed. The entry porch takes approximately 30% of the surface area, and the house, designed for a single person, consists simply of a glazed volume unequally divided by a timber box containing all services, the kitchen, bathroom, hi-fi and storage.

This house is the most original redefinition of the domestic interior this century. There is hardly an interior at all, with most furniture requirements assembled into one large piece which also acts as the back wall to each of the spaces. The front wall is the surrounding countryside.

The influence of the house has been enormous: in the treatment of kitchens and built-in furniture; in the proposition that a house can be a single architectural idea, and not a complex of them; in the clarity of construction and severity of detailing; in the way that service elements are held under tight rein. This house, unrepeatable as a series of any form, encapsulates Modernism's ability to invent icons.

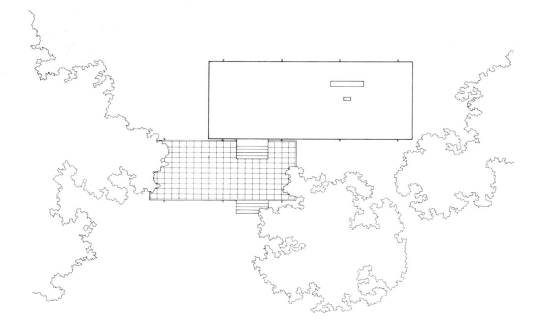

Site plan

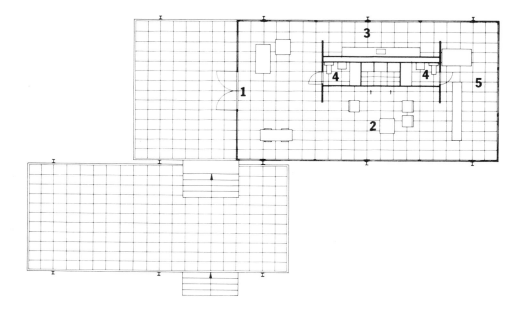

Plan

Exterior view

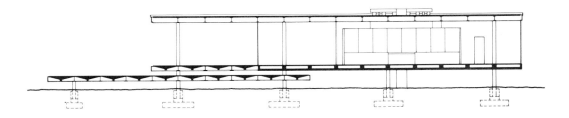

Long section plan

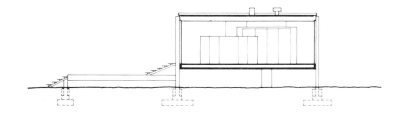

Cross section

Luis Barragán: Own House

To give a date to any house designed for himself by an architect is merely to give the point at which the house began to be used. Barragán has changed over time small features of the building but the basic organization has remained constant. The house is built in a street into which it slips unnoticed. The lot is divided by a wall one-third of the way along which separates Barragán's office from the house itself. Entrance to the house leads to a staircase hall. From here through the largest door the visitor enters a tall reception room. To the street side is a library but the major part of the room opens on to the garden. Above this floor are the bedrooms from which a narrow staircase leads to the roof terrace.

A zone in the middle of the house is given over to a complex of staircases, the spiral leading from the kitchen to the maid's suite on the roof.

None of this description gives any hint of the power and significance of the spaces. Barragán is perhaps one of the only architects to possess a surrealist sense of the construction of space.

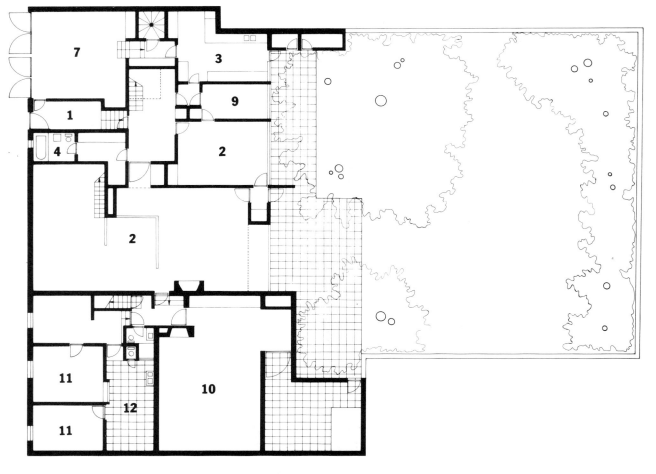

Ground floor plan

1 Entrance
2 Living room
3 Kitchen
4 Bathroom
5 Bedroom
6 Study
7 Garage
8 Terrace
9 Servants
10 Office
11 Storage
12 Plantroom

Drawn by Alex Fergusson

8

The quality of things as they are is inherent in his work; a staircase makes a nude descending float, jars standing in a patio appear like sentinels, and so on. The magic of the everyday, to make the familiar strange and the strange familiar is the core of this masterpiece.

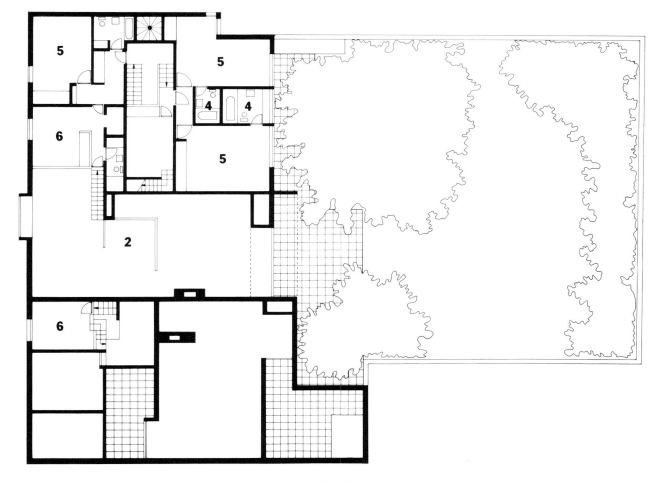

First floor plan

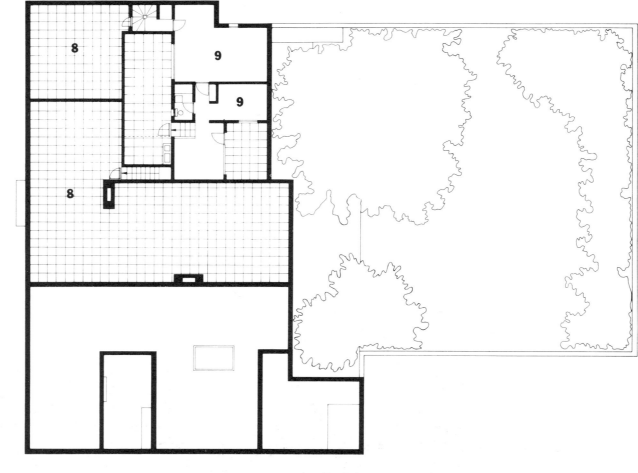

1 Entrance
2 Living room
3 Kitchen
4 Bathroom
5 Bedroom
6 Study
7 Garage
8 Terrace
9 Servants
10 Office
11 Storage
12 Plantroom

Roof plan

Living room

Patio

Bruce Goff: Ford House

1948

After 1945, the economic prosperity of the USA led many to commission individual houses. The work of Lloyd Wright in the pre-war period had now made of him an American hero, and that factor in turn had softened attitudes to what homes might look like. Goff's house would not have been built without a client who was prepared for a totally individual house.

Mrs Ford, a painter, wanted space to work in, to hang her work and to entertain. Goff's brilliant planning solution is to place the studio over the kitchen and dining alcove in the centre of the plan, with the living space curving around this. The living space includes an outdoor area within the circle, which is framed but not enclosed. The bedrooms are symmetrically deployed outside the circle with the buffer zone of closets and bathrooms acting as the transition space between.

The structure is a single load-bearing column, from which the circular studio is cantilevered over the kitchen/dining area. Ribs of steel lean against the column, and a skylight top-lighting the studio and flooding light into the living

Drawn by Luke Lowings

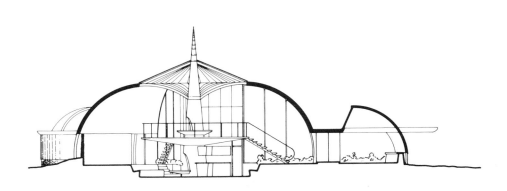

Section through carport

Ground floor plan

space is constructed as a diaphanous spire around the tapered column. The ribs are part of the Quonset steel prefabricated system which at the time of construction was being adapted from its wartime use to more general applications in industrial buildings.

Where the outdoor area bites into the circle of ribs, more light is provided by plate glass sliding doors. There are no opening windows in the buildings as such, all ventilation being provided by hinged timber louvres at the junction between the domical space and the enclosing walls at the base. These are made from coal, set in a random ashlar pattern with waste glass nuggets. The ceiling to the main space has cedar strips laid in a herringbone pattern.

Bathrooms have black terrazzo *in-situ* baths, ceilings of coiled rope and illumination through Plexiglas domes, made for bomber aircraft.

The geometry of the ribs dominates the house both internally and externally. The display of intelligently used but none the less mostly discarded materials gives the house a series of metaphors. At one level it is an ex-traordinary document to the vivacity of Goff's imagination that he could even think of employing such unconventional components, at another the desire to use the unusual is remarkably consistent with the strange forms he develops for the domestic interior.

1 Entrance
2 Living room
3 Kitchen
4 Bathroom
5 Bedroom
6 Terrace
7 Carport
8 Stairs to studio over

Exterior view

Richard Neutra: Warren Tremaine House

Following earlier experiments, Neutra achieved here an extraordinary degree of integration between construction, technical aspects and formal expression. The house is essentially a T-form plan with a lower level containing a gallery in a tunnel leading to a loggia, with a natural bowl to the south and swimming pool to the north.

The structure is a concrete frame carrying a cantilevered overhang so that the roof beam and slab sit upon the concrete frame as two distinct components. The space between the roof plate and the lintels of the frame contains openable windows for cross ventilation as well as artificial lighting. All windows are in aluminium frames directly fixed to the concrete. A plinth wall is constructed of stone.

The terrazzo of the house is terrazzo with electric coils planted beneath. The terrazzo extends from inside to outside, as does the heating, so that the users can sit outside in relative comfort on a chill evening. These constructional and technical details support a vision of the house framing the strong natural features

Drawn by Alex Fergusson

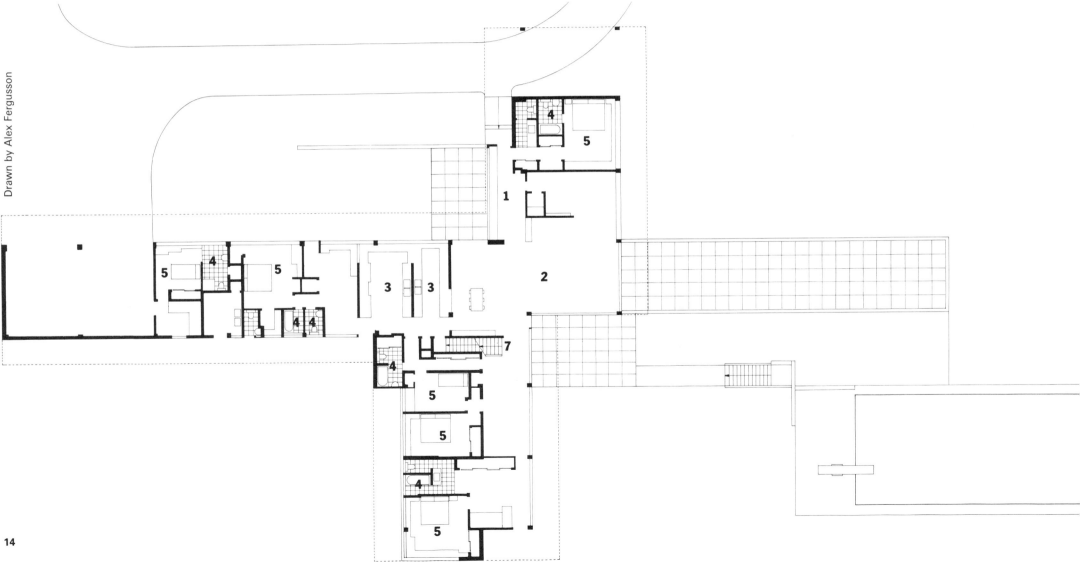

of the site, and, as in much of Lloyd Wright's work, contrasting man-made forms with the landscape. It is a house inconceivable outside its specific area which combines a European sensibility to materials with a dreamlike landscape.

1 Entrance
2 Living room
3 Kitchen
4 Bathroom
5 Bedroom
6 Office
7 Stairs down to pool
8 Swimming pool
9 Changing
10 Loggia

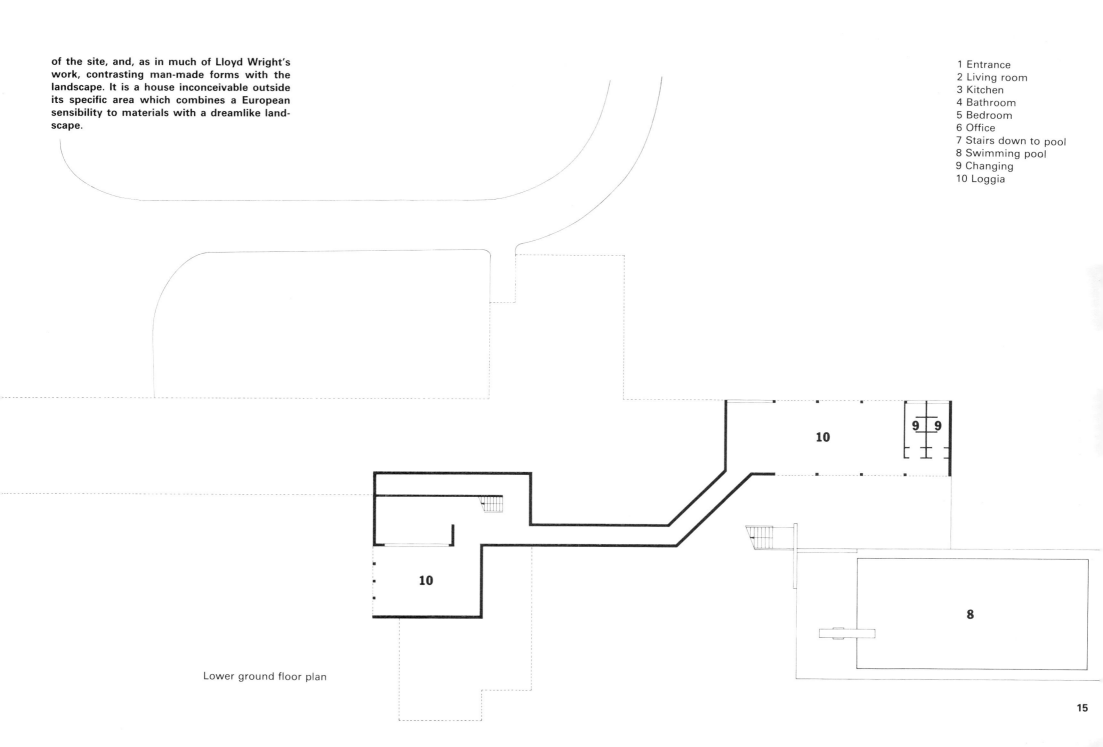

Lower ground floor plan

15

Charles Eames: Pacific Palisades

1949

The most creative architectural editor of this century in America was John Entenza. After the end of World War II he commissioned a series of houses for the Los Angeles based magazine, *Arts and Architecture*. Eames designed two of them which were built on adjacent lots, one for Eames' own use and next door a single-storey house for Entenza designed with Eero Saarinen (1910–1960).

Eames' house uses existing industrially made components in a straightforward and workmanlike way. But he uses the panelling necessary for an industrial grid in an inventive way. The exterior of his house consists of transparent panels, clear or wired glass; translucent panels which are glass fibre and opaque ones which are wood, grey asbestos, aluminium and coloured blue, red, earth colour, black or on occasion covered with plaster covered with gold leaf.

R. Craig Miller gives this description of the interior: 'In contrast to the starkness of many international style interiors, Eames' interiors were increasingly filled with distinctive ar-

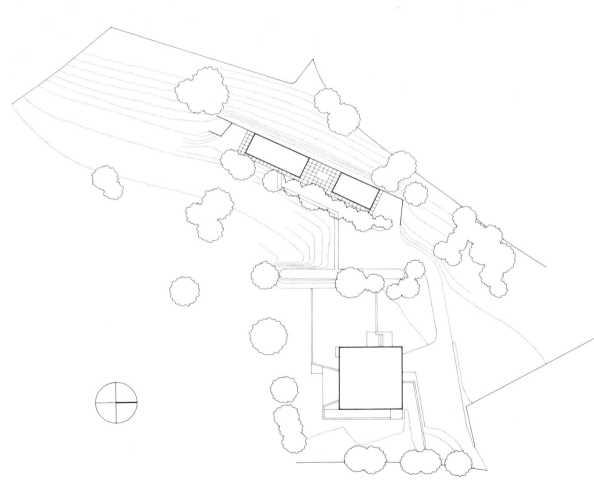

Site plan
Eames' house to the west, Entenza's to the east

1 Entrance
2 Living room
3 Kitchen
4 Bathroom
5 Bedroom
6 Study
7 Garage
8 Terrace

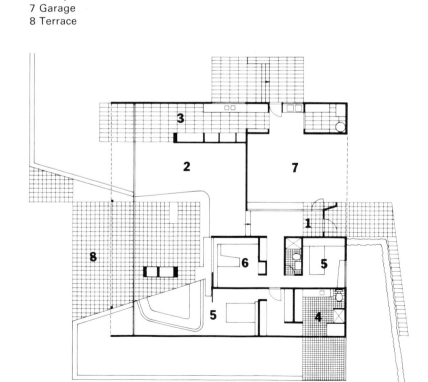

Entenza house
Ground floor plan

Drawn by Simon Colebrooke

16

rangements of furniture, rugs, flowers, pillows,
toys, candles, shells and other collectibles that
approached a high Victorian clutter.'

Garden elevation

1 Entrance
2 Living room
3 Kitchen
4 Bathroom
5 Bedroom
6 Terrace
7 Workshop
8 Storeroom
9 Void over

First floor plan

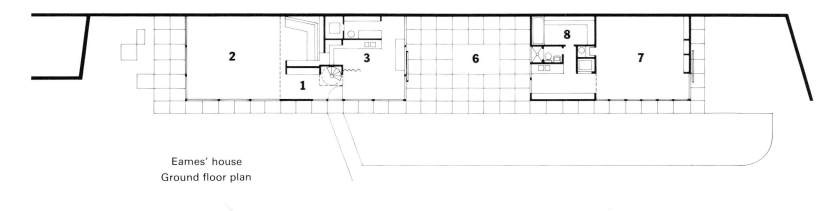

Eames' house
Ground floor plan

Ralph Erskine: House for Elof Nilsson

1949

Built for a manager of the paper mills in the same town, Erskine's first major house is an atrium-plan set within a 6 x 6 metre grid of timber-laminated columns. The roof slopes into the glazed atrium to use the collected snow as insulation during the winter. The atrium was to have been a winter garden but was turned to other uses as a music room by the occupants.

There are no external gutters, to avoid icicles forming. All roof drainage is internal. The various rationales for dealing with arctic extremes account for much of Erskine's detailing, but as with Aalto the rationales for the plan must be sought elsewhere. The atrium plan and separation of the parents' bedroom from those of the children may derive from the work of Cher-mayeff and Alexander: in any case the motives are similar.

But the bending of walls and forms used have more in common with the seeking of what became a strong theme in the arguments of Team X, that is for an erasure of the mechanical aspects of Modernism. This for Erskine derived from a deep humanism that gives pride of place

Drawn by Kate McCormack

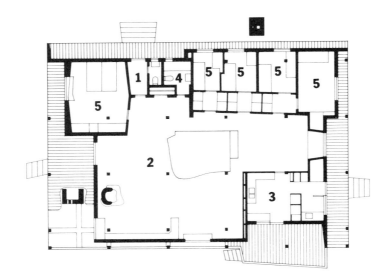

Ground floor plan

1 Entrance
2 Living room
3 Kitchen
4 Bathroom
5 Bedroom

to the celebration of the community life, while giving form to the individuals who compose any community. His buildings are like conversations between firmly held points of view, but not confrontations. In this plan, the roof shape and square plateau on which the building sits establish the mythical format for such a conversation.

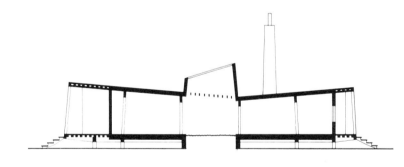

Section

Le Corbusier: House for Dr Curuchet

The site is surrounded by existing buildings on three sides while on the fourth side entry is made and there is a view on to a park. The brief called for a doctor's consulting suite and a three-bedroomed house.

Le Corbusier's sectional solution is to lift the consulting suite over the garage and entry, accessible only by a dog-leg ramp. At the half

landing the house can be entered and then a staircase rises to the living floor, now two floors above grade. The roof of the consulting suite serves as terrace for the living floor. Bedrooms are on the floor above.

A regular square grid of concrete columns runs from the front to the back. Brise-soleils, also in concrete, protect the continuous glazing

of the house and the consulting suite.

Various themes from the twenties are reworked in this extraordinary house. The use of pilotis permits the section. The promenade architectural is up the ramp, into the staircase hall, into the living room, with a corner cut away for a double-height space, and then out on to the partly roofed terrace. And in the

Drawn by Simon Colebrooke

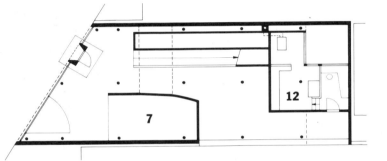

Ground floor plan

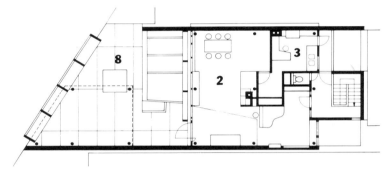

Second floor plan

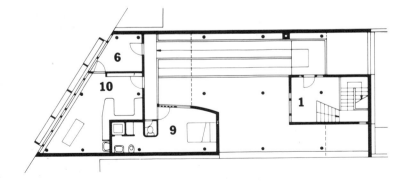

First floor plan

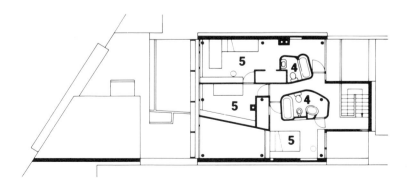

Third floor plan

20

planning of the bedroom floor, the ideas of the free plan are frozen into the soft curves surrounding the bathrooms.

But the greatest impact of this house depends upon an almost decorative use of structure, so that progression along the promenade is through spaces which are closed, and open, with short views and long vistas. The building hints at a mysterious ceremony of invitation.

Street elevation

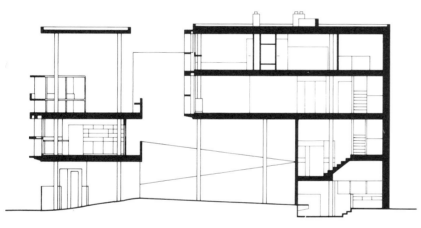

Long section through the surgery

1 Entrance
2 Living room
3 Kitchen
4 Bathroom
5 Bedroom
6 Surgery entrance
7 Garage
8 Terrace
9 Servants
10 Surgery

Interior of entrance

Frank Lloyd Wright: Price House

1951

Built for the owners of the Price tower in Bartlesville, Oklahoma, the Price is one of Frank Lloyd Wright's longest houses, and said to be the last he personally supervised before his death. The site rises gently and the house lifts with it from a garage court along a corridor to a central three-bay square space. This is the living room, open to the dry desert air, but roofed

to protect the room from direct sunlight. Beyond it, a further corridor slips past the fireplace to a range of four bedrooms designed to accommodate the large Price family.

A servants' wing is located next to the garages in the entry court. Construction is of standard concrete blocks, as are many of Wright's Arizona houses. The blocks are laid in courses

that set back $\frac{1}{2}$ inch per course. Wright designed most of the furniture here. The plan of the house is a truncated pin wheel, not dissimilar to the Robie house. But aspect is toward the garden to the north with the corridor on the south side, with views out to the grid of Phoenix across the desert.

Wright grasped the climate here as a major

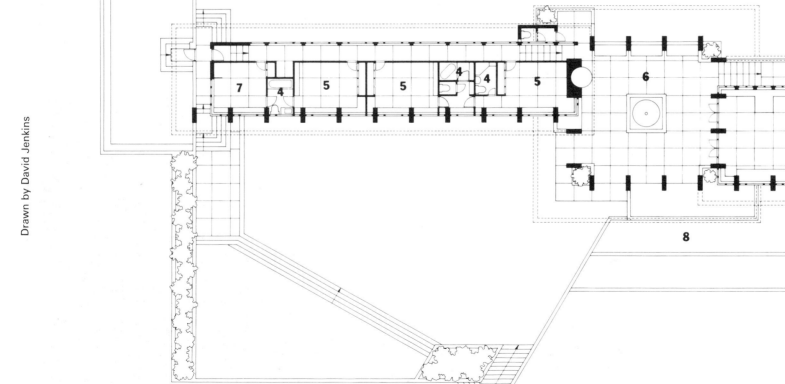

Drawn by David Jenkins

Ground floor plan

1 Entrance
2 Living room
3 Kitchen
4 Bathroom
5 Bedroom
6 Outdoor living room
7 Guest bedroom
8 Garden

generator in ways that few of his other houses do. The house's structure seems to grow out of the desert and forms a saw-tooth joint with the timber roof and glazing. In the central living room the structural piers taper to their bases, and the roof, supported on steel pins, appears to float. The world enclosed is clear, bright and secure.

Entrance

Living room

Alvar Aalto: Summerhouse

1953

Aalto's lakeside cottage breaks the European tradition of the house by using it as a testbed for materials. This theme can also be found in Le Corbusier's apartment for himself and his wife on top of his rue Nungessor-et-Coli block where Le Corbusier experimented with forms and materials. Play with materials is also a theme in buildings by Frank Lloyd Wright and by Bruce Goff.

The scheme consists of rooms arranged around a courtyard, a big drawing studio and then bedrooms. The courtyard is lined with panels of various ceramic and timber surfaces and was built to test the durability of the various materials. The house then continues in fragmentary form with a series of gazebo-like objects down to the lake. The theme of the decay of a form, or perhaps more accurately the extension in fragments of a form, was also to have been developed in the Town Hall at Saynatsalo (1949–1952), but the blocks beyond the Town Hall itself were never built.

The personal nature of Aalto's work inspired many who could not follow the formal wizardry

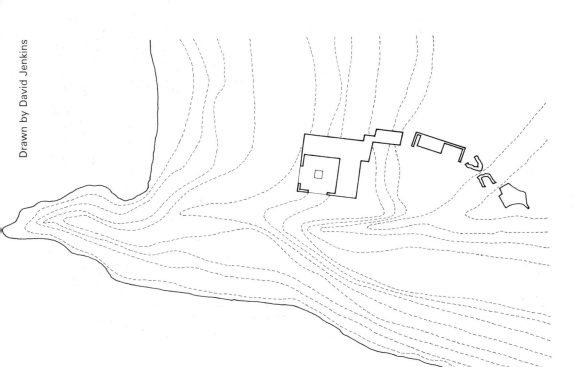

Drawn by David Jenkins

Site plan

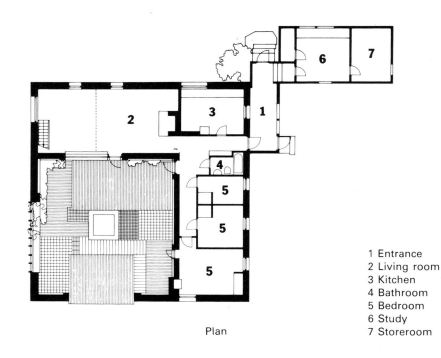

Plan

1 Entrance
2 Living room
3 Kitchen
4 Bathroom
5 Bedroom
6 Study
7 Storeroom

of Le Corbusier at Ronchamp. Aalto seemed to provide an overriding rationale which was then embroidered with a set of gestures, also in retrospect themselves part of a repertoire. This double system could be extended from the site plan into the furniture and light fittings, which are perhaps the *jeu d'esprit* of the whole *oeuvre*.

At Muuratsalo, constructed a year after his second marriage, the controlling force is the courtyard, usually a negative form. It is as if the process of construction has finally come out on top of the Modernist dream of forms that transform society.

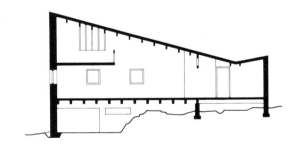

Section

View into courtyard

Philip Johnson: Wiley House

1953

Johnson, as Mies' disciple then apostate, has suffered more from his own taste for self-publicity than any other American. The buildings are obscured by his cascade of wit. But in the 1950s when, eclectic as ever, he borrowed from those more talented than himself, he produced a series of houses which experimented with the Miesian formulations of a house.

The Wiley house puts the glass box on a podium. That is the simple and beautiful point of this design. The podium houses all 'private functions' in a workmanlike way, and elegantly grows out of the site. The glass box/pavilion then sits on the podium, the public space of the house. The formula consists of a fixed element, the glass box, and a variable element, the podium, which the client extended by 6 feet during the course of construction, 'injuring the proportions not in the slightest', according to the architect.

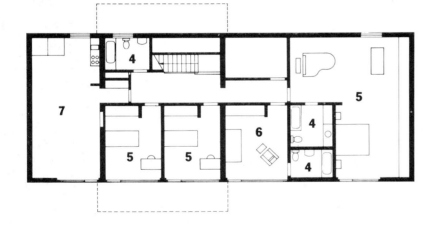

Ground floor plan

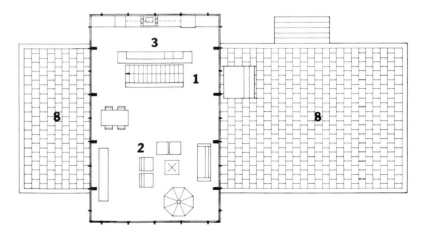

First floor plan

Drawn by Penny Gibson

26

1 Entrance
2 Living room
3 Kitchen
4 Bathroom
5 Bedroom
6 Study
7 Den
8 Terrace

Exterior view

Oscar Niemeyer: Own House
1953

This, the second house built by Niemeyer for himself (for the first see Volume 1), is situated on an equally dramatic site. Here, however, the house's section is sharply divided between a base, used for sleeping, and cut into the earth, and the living areas, which occupy the pavilion above.

The debt to Le Corbusier is clear, one lives *par*

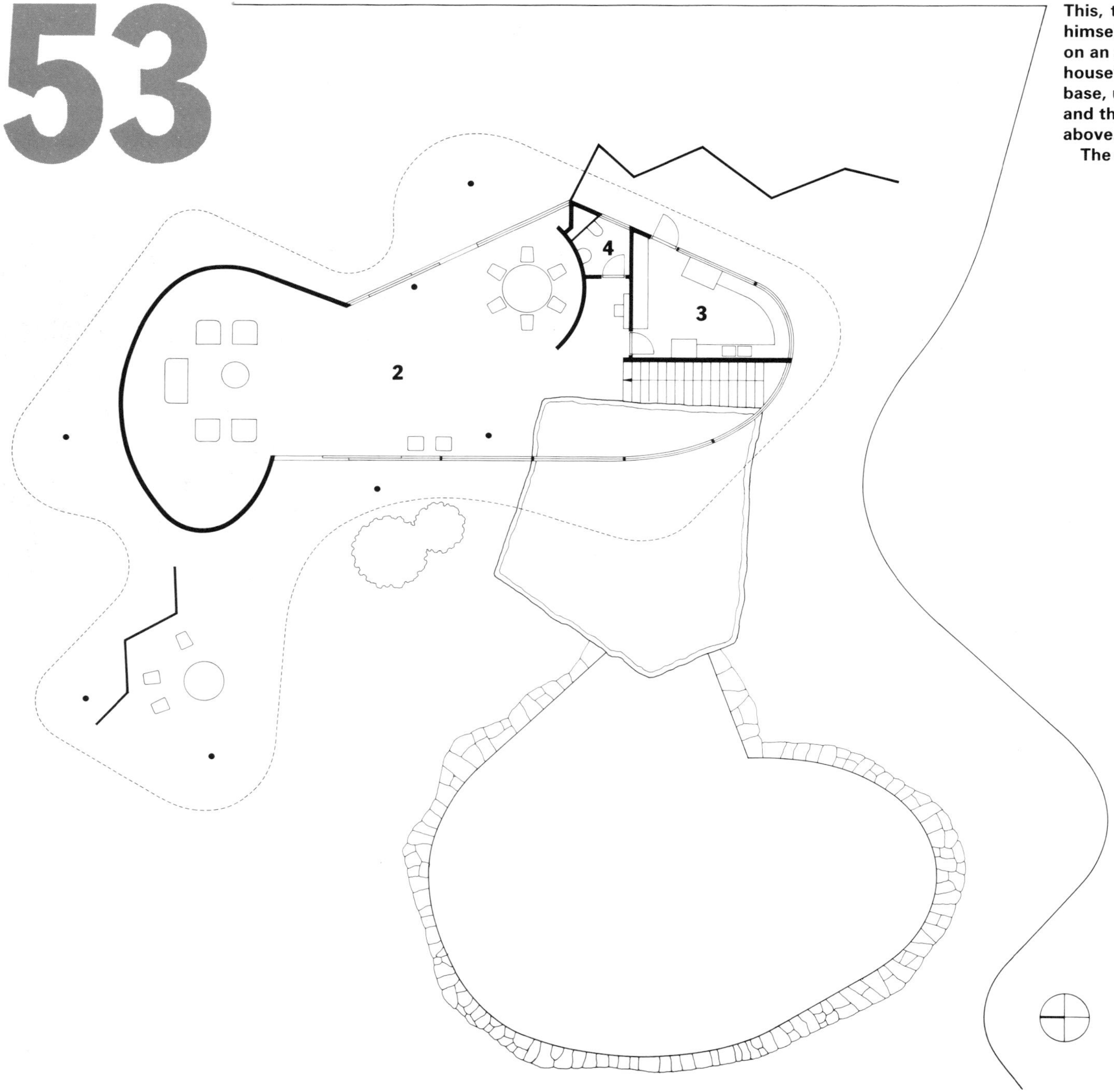

Drawn by David Jenkins

1 Entrance
2 Living room
3 Kitchen
4 Bathroom
5 Bedroom
6 Study

Upper floor plan

étage, but the amoebic volume occurred in the master's work only with respect to services up to this time. The interpenetration of the exterior into the interior is total, due perhaps more to the examples of Neutra and Frank Lloyd Wright.

This living floor is the proposition of free space in two lights: free in the sense that within one volume the various activities are dispose, free in the sense that nothing impedes passage from exterior to interior. The overall form is a metaphor for nature, could be organic, could even be free. Indeed it could also be said to derive from the forms used by Roberto Burle Marx in his landscape designs and reminds one now rather a little too much of the kidney-shaped pool so beloved of tourism and suburbia.

In any case, structure has ceased to be any kind of determinant, though it would be impossible to conceive this house without steel. But structure as some logic which dictates and orders form is totally subordinated to formal considerations alone. The house stands as an idea of shelter, to be generously interpreted as the pavilion above the caves.

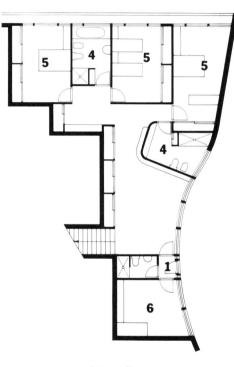

Lower floor plan

Pool level

Jorn Utzon: House at Hellebæk

Utzon was a student of both Kay Fisker and Steen Eiler Rasmussen at the Academy of Fine Arts in Copenhagen. He worked for Aalto and for Gunnar Asplund. From these powerful forces promoting the development of Modernism in Scandinavia it will be no surprise to see that this house is a rigorous and elemental composition.

The house is approached from a car port/pergola with brick walls either side and the roof timbers of the house stretched between them. This signals the compositional method of the house. Enclosure is formed between elements – walls, roof plane, windows – upon a base. Each element has a certain autonomy. Thus the timber lining to the walls of the living room touches neither floor nor ceiling. Where there might have been a skirting or ceiling moulding, Utzon provides a recess from the timber lining back to the surface of the substrate. Similarly, all brickwork is finished with a soldier course as if these walls were part of a garden. The base of the building is lined with brick: later this element would receive more

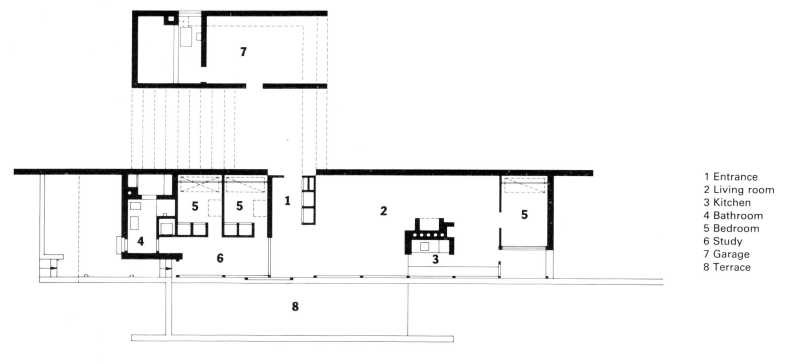

Ground floor plan

1 Entrance
2 Living room
3 Kitchen
4 Bathroom
5 Bedroom
6 Study
7 Garage
8 Terrace

Drawn by Penny Gibson

attention from Utzon.

In *Architecture in an Age of Scepticism* (Heinemann, London, 1984), Utzon characterized all three projects published there as houses. Sydney Opera House is 'a house of festivals', the Kuwait National Assembly Complex is 'a house for work and decisions' and his vacation in Spain is 'a house for family life'. Few other architects have the courage to be that rigorous. The house at Hellebaek is the first stage in the process.

Terrace

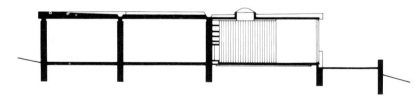

Cross-section

Le Corbusier: House for Mrs Manorama Sarabhai

From Le Corbusier's commentary it is clear that not all went well with the project – he objects to the use of fans in the house, and to the reduced size of the proposed swimming pool, for example. Nevertheless the house as constructed is a magnificent structure of parallel load-bearing walls roofed by catalan vaults whose upper surface is grassed and watered to provide a garden. The plan divides into four parts. A garage, a servant's wing, including kitchen, Mrs Sarabhai's quarters and a separate apartment for her son.

Given the extensive use of open verandahs it is hard to decipher interior from exterior. This is clearly not a house that could be protected by steel shutters. The grain established by the vaults suggests a series of tunnels but the dispositions of load-bearing walls and slab columns allows a variety of spaces, especially in the dining space and living room, where the transverse dimension dominates.

The materials are local: roughly made bricks in beds of thick mortar, rough concrete lintels and beams, and a floor of Madras stone laid in a

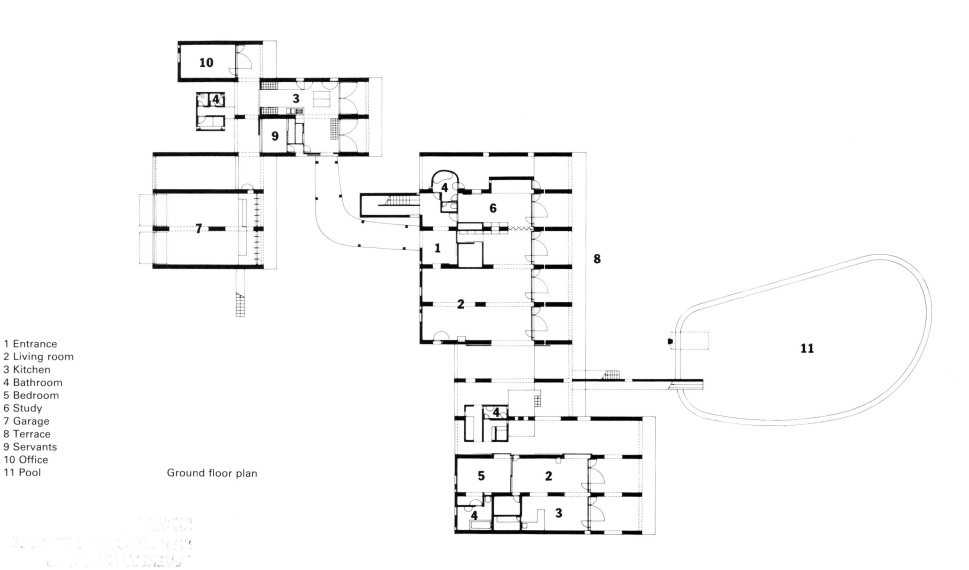

Drawn by Luke Lowings

1 Entrance
2 Living room
3 Kitchen
4 Bathroom
5 Bedroom
6 Study
7 Garage
8 Terrace
9 Servants
10 Office
11 Pool

Ground floor plan

modular pattern playing a riff against the longitudinal dynamics of the vaults.

Ultimately the house has no exterior; it simply stops when need dictates and perhaps thereby the free plan is translated into a free form. Few architects could have seen the chance of disposing of so many western spatial prejudices.

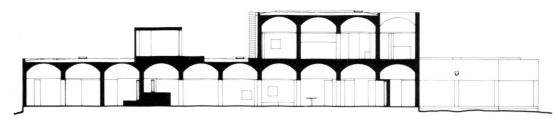

Section

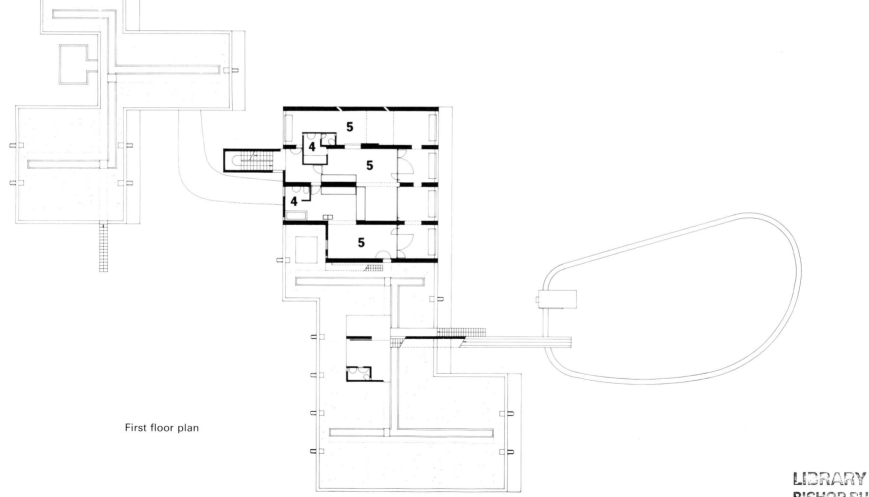

First floor plan

Alison and Peter Smithson: Sugden House

Meeting the Smithsons through working for the structural engineers, Ove Arup and Partners, Mr Sugden commissioned a 1750 square foot freestanding house at Watford, near London. It has remained in the same hands since completion with few alterations. Superficially the external materials speak of houses of the suburbs, second-hand London stocks with standard metal windows, dark red tiles, a pitched roof.

As Vincent Scully points out in *The Shingle Style of Today* (Yale University Press, New Haven, 1971), this house and Stirling and Gowan's contemporary works re-establish vernacular materials in the modern tradition.

The plan and section, however, differ wildly from the surrounding buildings. The ground floor is virtually one large L-shaped room, with a higher ceiling over the living room part. The pitch of the roof in the four bedrooms above is revealed so that each room extends into the volume enclosed by the roof; there are no suspended ceilings.

Then the variety of the elevation relates directly to the uses of the rooms, to view and

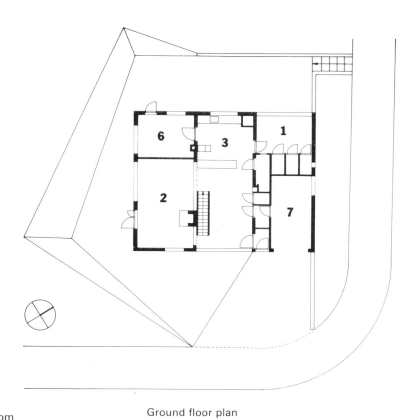

Ground floor plan

First floor plan

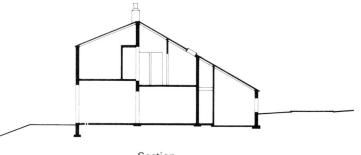

Section

1 Entrance
2 Living room
3 Kitchen
4 Bathroom
5 Bedroom
6 Study
7 Garage

orientation, although hints of a disjointed symmetry can be found, especially in the north-east and south-west facades. This home, unduly neglected by architectural critics and theorists, establishes a loose-limbed, easy way of accommodating both high art and mass culture. The disciplines of the plan, three equal zones of space partially separated by load-bearing walls, barely registers at first glance. The customary heavy-handedness of English moral modern taste slackens, and a wider perspective akin to the *architecture autre* more polemically advanced by Rayner Banham in The New Brutalism (Architectural Press, London, 1966) opens out from this rich mixture.

Living room

Garden elevation

Jean Prouvé: Prototype House for L'Abbé Pierre

1956

It is not clear how many examples of this house still exist. Dominique Layssen (in *Jean Prouvé, L'idée constructive*, Dunod, Paris, 1983), suggests that a dozen examples still exist in France, and shows pictures of a recent reconstruction by J.P. Levasseur. The house was originally designed for Abbé Pierre, who had appealed to Prouvé to design a dwelling to solve the post-war housing crisis in France. The solution took 6 weeks to design and produce, cost 150 000 old francs and took less than 7 hours to erect on a site on the *quai* in Paris. Money was raised for the project through a scheme using coupons on Persil detergent packets.

The plan of the dwelling measures 8.77 metres by 6.31 metres. The floor area is 52 square metres. The structural core of the house is the service core, which carries a steel beam on to which the roof is superimposed.

The sequence of erection is

1. Cast the base in concrete which is raised to form a continuous ledge at seat level inside the house.

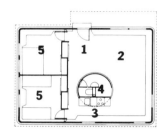

Plan

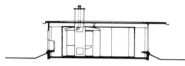

Two sections

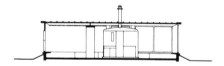

2. Lift into position the service core and position the steel beam.
3. Superimpose the roof structure.
4. Enclose the space with wall panels made of two layers of bakelized wood between which is a 5 cm core of polystyrene.

The project demanded that there be no circulation space as such so as to maximize the space available for the living area. The consequence of this idea and the design of the service core as a single structural core means that the lavatory opens directly into the living space. This, though not uncommon in French apartments, gave the Ministry enough reason to ignore the project.

1 Entrance
2 Living room
3 Kitchen
4 Bathroom
5 Bedroom

James Stirling and James Gowan: House at Cowes

1956

This small house was for a couple and their two children. The plan on a 5 x 5 foot grid reserves one wing for bedrooms, the other for living rooms, with kitchen and bathroom joining the link. Construction is of white fairfaced brickwork for external structural walls and 2½-inch-thick fairfaced concrete block for non-load-bearing partitions. Windows in timber frames are based on the golden section. The building comes during the design and construction of the flats at Ham Common 1955–1958, and can be seen as a cooler variant on them. Cooler in the sense that the excitement of Jaoul is tempered by a constructional logic, and cooler in the classical simplicity of the plans of the Isle of Wight house. If there was to be some return to axial planning at this time, then the whole apparatus of the Beaux Arts could not ride through the chink. The most obvious way out was to design within the dimensional constraints and constructional practice of building elements. Later and lesser architects would raise this solution to a moral imperative and become blindly involved with the nature of

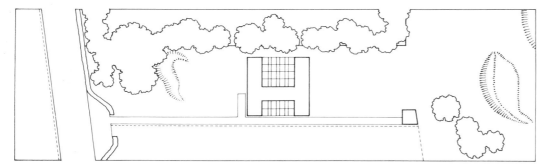

Site plan

Plan

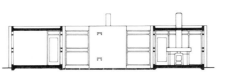

Section

1 Entrance
2 Living room
3 Kitchen
4 Bathroom
5 Bedroom
6 Study

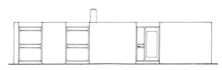

Elevation

materials, as if anything mass-produced could have a Platonic essence.

This small, practical and plain building offered another route to a twentieth-century vernacular.

West elevation

Living room

Atelier 5: Merz House
1958

Resembling an early project for the Villa Stein, with the 'service' wing extending towards the entrance to form an entry court, this house is one of the most extreme cases of single-storey living raised to the power of a three-storey house. The ground is effectively raised on pilotis, the storage and laundry space taking up some volume. The service wing consists of garages and a studio. The main floor is a long apartment completely glazed to the view and south-facing side. From the entrance level with bedroom, changing and bathrooms *en suite*, the visitor is led to the dining room, separated from the living room by the fireplace wall, and then to the terrace.

An external staircase leads up to the roof garden which at the entrance end has two smaller bedrooms.

If there is an architectural promenade here it is between structure and view. The house is a long thin walk masking that view and the structure operates both pragmatically and as gesture. Any looking away from the Corbusian programme is more than compensated for by

Roof garden

Site plan

an exquisite mastery of concrete as it is used for column, frame, solid wall and in all places the memory of the wood from which it has been struck. The weathering qualities of concrete in this rural setting, encouraging lichen and a patina of wear, contrast with the precision of glass.

Atelier 5 were the first European architects to establish their reputation on a repertoire of housing. They advanced beyond the design of houses for experimental purposes to the kind relation between their understanding of the tradition of Modernism and their sympathy with site and purpose.

Entrance view

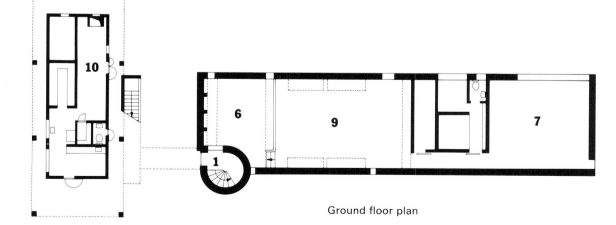

Ground floor plan

1 Entrance
2 Living room
3 Kitchen
4 Bathroom
5 Bedroom
6 Study
7 Garage
8 Terrace
9 Studio
10 Storage

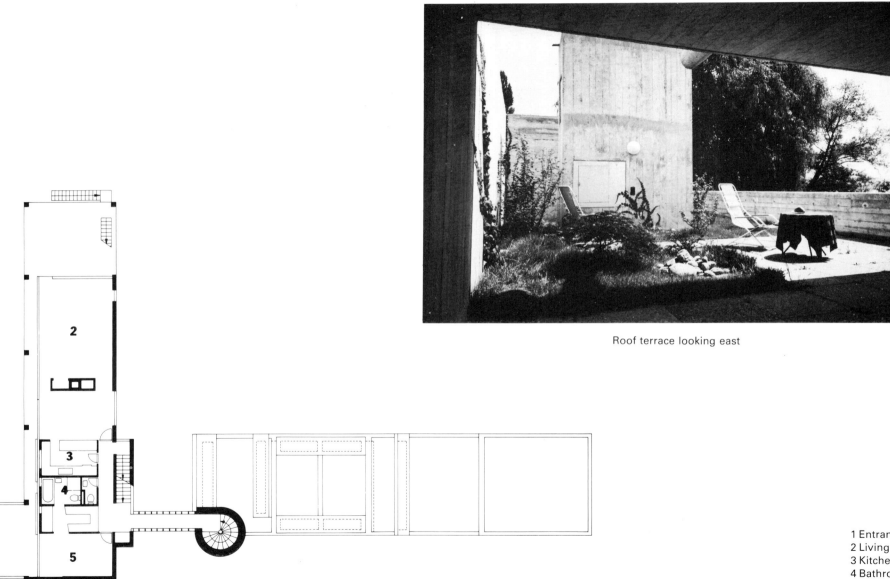

Roof terrace looking east

First floor plan

1 Entrance
2 Living room
3 Kitchen
4 Bathroom
5 Bedroom
6 Study
7 Garage
8 Terrace
9 Studio
10 Storage

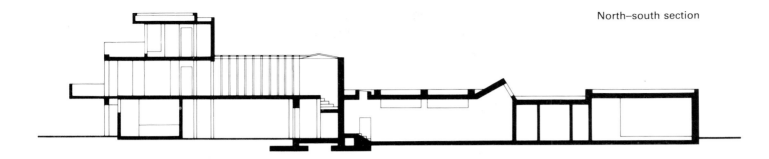

North–south section

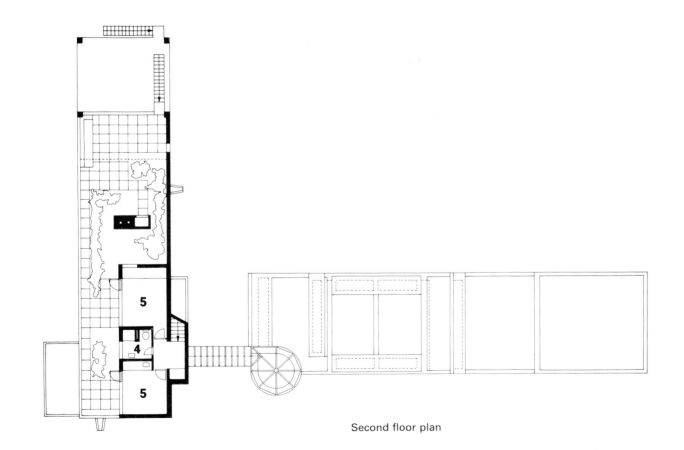

Second floor plan

O. M. Ungers: Own House

1958

While Ungers is now thought of primarily as an architect of large-scale schemes, of which the Frankfurt Messe is still the only completed example, his early career in the fifties in and around Cologne was substantially based upon housing. The two houses next to the Berlin Wall, and, most exciting, the House within a House designed for the Houses for Sale exhibition held at the Castelli Gallery, New York are strong conceptions of new types.

At Cologne, the house ends a terrace of ample but dreary suburban houses. From the outside the powerful facades present few clues to the light interior which opens to the garden. The ground floor of the house is Ungers' office and a self-contained flat. The upper floor is the family home. The house has a severe front, brick, concrete, lintels and strip windows. This reading of the urban function of a facade is one that Ungers, and the Howard house, state most clearly, and was widely held at the time. But Ungers' plan is composed of rooms. Spaces do not flow one into another, and for this reason alone Ungers must be reckoned one of the first

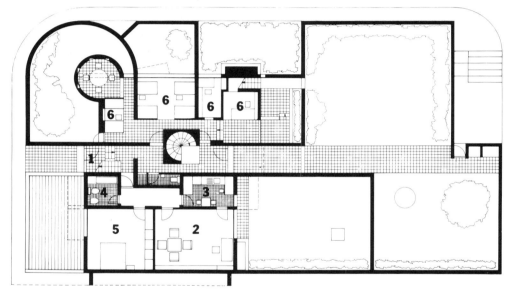

Ground floor plan

First floor plan

Drawn by Penny Gibson

1 Entrance
2 Living room
3 Kitchen
4 Bathroom
5 Bedroom
6 Office

Europeans, along with Rossi, to recognize the importance of Loos.

In later works the elementarist compositional technique has developed into a refined series of experiments with typology confronting systematic design. The house he built for himself with originally two other apartments now brought into the service of the Ungers family contains the generative seeds from which the later work springs. Anyone doubting this need only consult the magnificent visual commentary, *Sieben Variationen des Raumes uber die Sieben leuchter des Baukunst von John Ruskin* (Verlag Gerd Hatje, Stuttgart, 1985), written and assembled by Ungers.

Street elevation

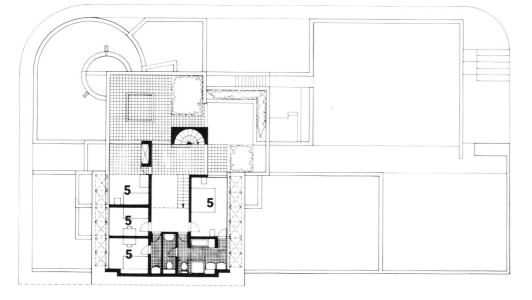

Second floor plan

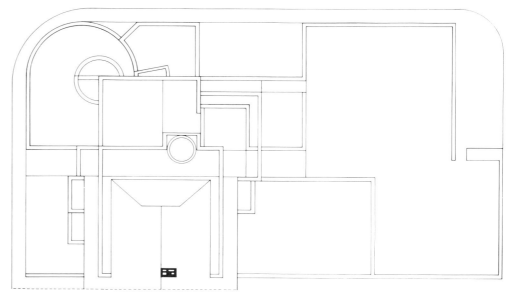

Roof plan

Edward Cullinan: Marvin House

1959

Self-build in Califormia is associated with communes and what can be rescued from builders' tips. Cullinan's could not be more different. He has described this house as 'five glass-topped concrete masonry towers...placed beside...a long gallery'. There is a space for a bed at the landside end, then a lounge space and a dining room next to the kitchen.

The house consists of two parts, the solid service areas and the timber and glass gallery. What differentiates the house from others is that it is set end on to the view, with the gallery facing south. In the original scheme a road was to have been cut coming directly down the hill, as the grid streets do in San Francisco.

In thinking of the house as self-build, the crucial element is the junction between glazed roof and pitch, resolved here by a typical direction of post-war architecture – to enlarge a detail beyond its normal size while retaining the original function *and* doubling that with another, here the continuous beam on to which the gallery roof sits, which is also a gutter, which is also the cupboard zone of the house.

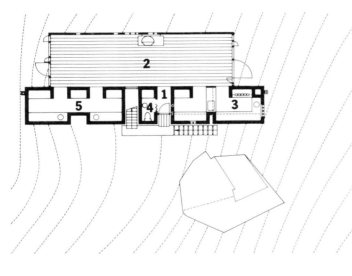

Plan

1 Entrance
2 Living room
3 Kitchen
4 Bathroom
5 Bedroom

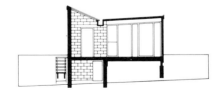

Section

46

Exterior

Interior

Egon Eierman: Own House

1959

Eierman's own home for his family, ranging in age from 3 to 83 years, tries to give each member of the family their own space. The site on the edge of the Schlossberg slopes 7 metres across the site which gives the garden around which the house focuses a strong character. The building actually lines the street, alongside which lies the main entrance, and contains garages, a workroom and above a separate guest apartment. The main body of the house splits along its length to give a stepped section.

A cross wall at 4-metre centres disciplines the plan while the elevations continue, at domestic scale, the exoskeletal framework which for Eierman almost became a signature in his later works.

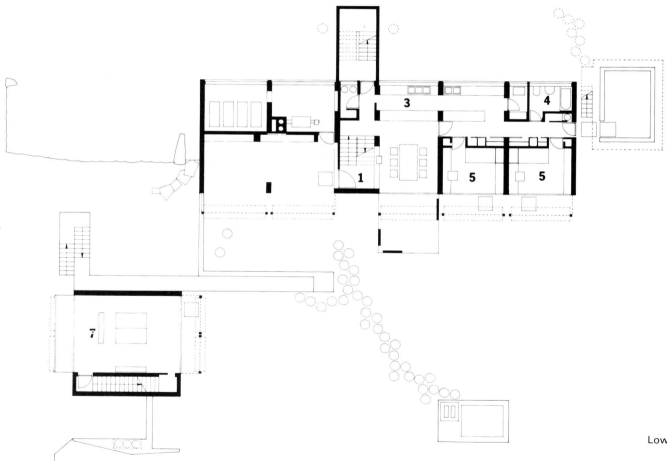

Lower floor plan

1 Entrance
2 Living room
3 Kitchen
4 Bathroom
5 Bedroom
6 Study
7 Garage

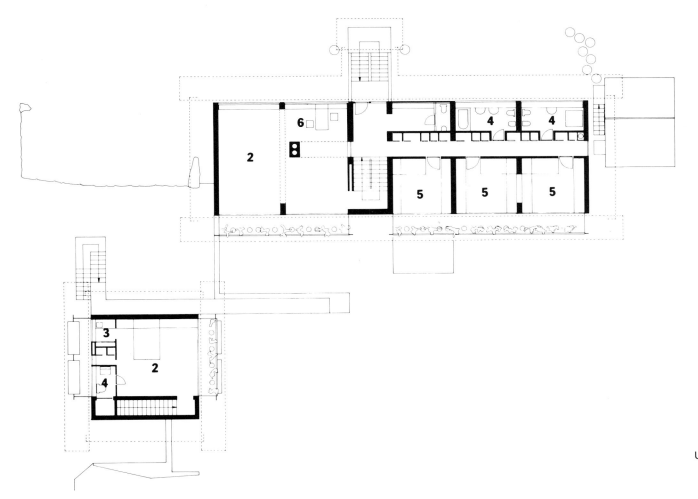

Upper floor plan

John Voelcker: House at Arkley

1960

From the road all this house presents the visitor is a garage door and barred gate. This is the entry to the private courtyard of the house. The angle of the garden wall leads and points to the corner of the house where the real front door is. Through that, in the vestibule is a curved wall with a photo-mural by John McHale that adds *trompe l'oeil* pilasters to the lavatory door

frame. To the left lies the living room and studio beyond, divided from each other by a wall generated from the entry wall position. To the right is the dining room/kitchen, playroom and then a suite of four bedrooms. The house is constructed of Wessex dark multi-bricks, with cedar shingles on the roof. Doors and panels are varnished ply. Floor finishes change from

wood block in the living room, clay tiles elsewhere, except the bedroom wing which is cork tiled.

The courtyard of the house has a framed appearance on two sides, with a brick wall and high-level windows on the south-west wall of the bedroom wing. Elsewhere small windows are punched for view, or high-level windows

Drawn by Alex Fergusson

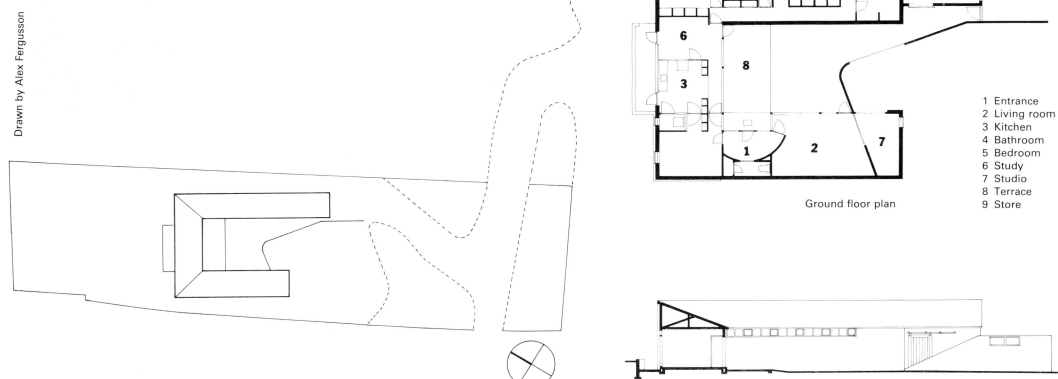

1 Entrance
2 Living room
3 Kitchen
4 Bathroom
5 Bedroom
6 Study
7 Studio
8 Terrace
9 Store

Ground floor plan

North–south section

Site plan

give sunlight to the living room, which faces north-east.

The vigour of the plan, section and construction which this house exhibits is one path, following perhaps the earlier experiments of Taylor and Green, to establishing a modern vernacular. There are few tricks, the *trompe* being the wittiest, and good practice dictates the detailing. The elevations result from two pressures – the nature of the rooms behind, and a minimal expression through proper use of materials. The house is so quiet as to almost pass unnoticed.

Entrance into courtyard

Entrance elevation

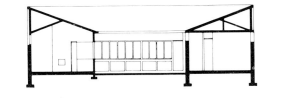

East–west section

West elevation

Louis I. Kahn: Esherick House

1961

Kahn built relatively few houses. In each there seems to be a larger-scale building trying to escape from the confines of the client's budget. In the Esherick House, the inherent monumentality of the plan is diminished by the fact that the major living spaces are surrounded by very thick walls. In the double-height living room, the fireplace wall is literally deep. The opposite wall in plan also has a fireplace used in the bathroom, but the wall is thicker containing a zone of servant spaces, kitchen, bathrooms, closets which are not part of the axial symmetry of the two major living spaces. The two window walls are also thick but these frame walls with alcoves or niches between the casements. The most intricate planning occurs on the first floor where the sliding doors between the gallery and bedroom, and then between bedroom and bathroom, suggest a flow of space from void to room to altar.

It is not, however, a free plan in any sense despite the double-height space. Each room is contained in the possible position of furniture by strong bi-axial synthesis. In that sense it is

1 Entrance
2 Living room
3 Kitchen
4 Bathroom
5 Bedroom
6 Store
7 Void over living room

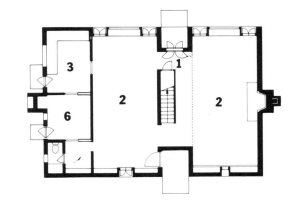

Ground floor plan

First floor plan

hardly an American house at all, relating more closely to an engorged church or tempietto than to the loose-limbed planning at which American architects seem adept. If freedoms are allowed they would reside more in the complex proportions of the major rooms.

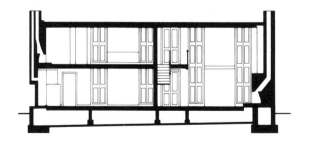

Section

Garden elevation

Charles Moore: Own House

1962

Moore's first house for himself was constructed at the same time as the founding of his practice, Moore, Lyndon Turnball Whitaker, when he was Chairman of the Architecture School at Berkeley. He has recorded the practice's facination with Summerson's essay, 'Heavenly mansions: an interpretation of Gothic' (in J. Summerson, *Heavenly Mansions and Other Essays*

on Architecture, (Architectural Press, London, 1949). From there Moore argued that the aedicule is a symbolic shelter, from time immemorial.

At Orinda, on a one-acre site behind San Francisco Bay, Moore constructed a barn-like frame inside which eight 10-foot-high Tuscan columns of solid fir define the living space and a shower. A false pyramidal ceiling resting on

either pair of four columns is painted internally, and the apex is crowned by a rooflight. The enclosing square has each corner cut away for glazing, or sliding doors which roll away. The base of the house is a concrete plinth with brick laid on top.

The house consists of two aedicules within a shelter. A w.c. and closet are on the 'servant'

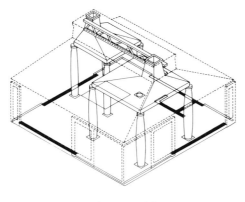

Axonometric

Ground floor plan

side of the square, following Kahn's distinction between servant and served spaces. This was one of the first uses of columns to define space as opposed to the use of columns in modern architecture to express structure. As such the other innovation to be seen involved bringing the shower and submerged bath into the living space, albeit on the servant side of the house.

This trick, possible only in a bachelor's accommodation, both ritualizes washing as a semi-public function but also suggests the uses of fountains and pools in Roman atrium houses.

From simplicity derive the greatest ambiguities. Later a full height bookcase was added, dividing the sleeping area, which begins to compromise the original simplicity. Nevertheless the forming of views, play of light and grandeur of the original idea are what makes this house a Modernist experiment.

1 Entrance
2 Living room
3 Kitchen
4 Bath
5 Bedroom

Robert Venturi and John Rauch: Mother's House

1962

The house was originally built by Venturi for his mother. It has since her death changed hands but is well kept by its present occupants. Venturi designed a series of houses at this time, some grand like the project of Millard Meiss, others minute, like the Frug.

What makes this a masterpiece is the overall composition and the exciting spatial events. No two rooms are the same in shape or section. The bounding rectangle and the wide gable are both sufficiently large to give a simple shape which Venturi then erodes. The greatest effort is at the spatial junction of the entrance, the staircase and the fireplace. Here the play of light and shadow, of reflections on glass, of layer and volume, of view and privacy of ordinariness and allusion are all under powerful control.

Their interaction with each other provokes a restlessness which is juxtaposed with the simple domesticity of the living area. There is no single meaning to this juxtaposition. The visitor is left spellbound by the invention. What is contradicted is the dumb simple-mindedness

Drawn by Alex Fergusson and David Jenkins

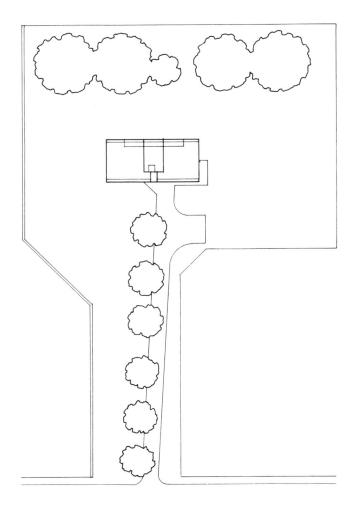

Site plan

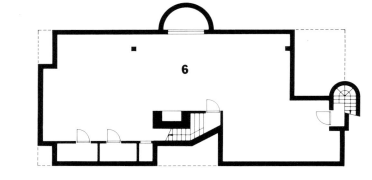

Basement plan

1 Entrance
2 Living room
3 Kitchen
4 Bathroom
5 Bedroom
6 Den

Ground floor plan

of Modernism's imitators. There is too some extent of a free plan, with an amount of zoning of types of space. But the overall strength of the plan and section holds two ideas in tension: that of the economical plan where no gesture is wasted, and that of the domestic tradition for the nineteenth century, a wide roof, a staircase hall, and much light.

Venturi's own description of the house plays up the deliberate formal complexities and does not describe the elegance or simplicity of his design. For him it was a polemical gesture against the house designed to express and expose the nature of materials, and the logic of construction. At no point in this house is the visitor bothered by such self-advertisement.

The spaces produced and their formal interplay dominate construction and materials without effort. The design work was so difficult that none have successfully copied the intricacies and advanced beyond the skill shown here.

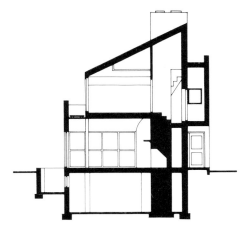

Long section

Cross section

First floor plan

Entrance elevation

James Gowan: Schreiber House
1964

On most of the roads bordering Hampstead Heath, large villas were constructed from about 1930 to 1960. Those houses reflect the growth of a village around a spa, which was Hampstead as the affluent moved in. Moreover, the desire to look over the greatest park in London not only offers obvious delights but reinforces that country house ownership dream of the rising bourgeoisie.

Since 1945 little of any real distinction was built until the Schreiber House of 1964. Unlike its nooky neighbours, Gowan's design is a castlee of five towers constructed in blue engineering bricks with the glazing offering few clues as to the scale of the interior. If the castle is one predominant lineage, the other rationale is the dimensions of materials used. The interior follows a strict module in the floor, the plaster-panelled walls and the coffered ceiling. This dimensional clarity, not achievable in cheaper construction, is the sign of the luxuriousness of the house.

Compositional elements such as the kitchen, bathrooms and staircases are spectacularly

Site plan

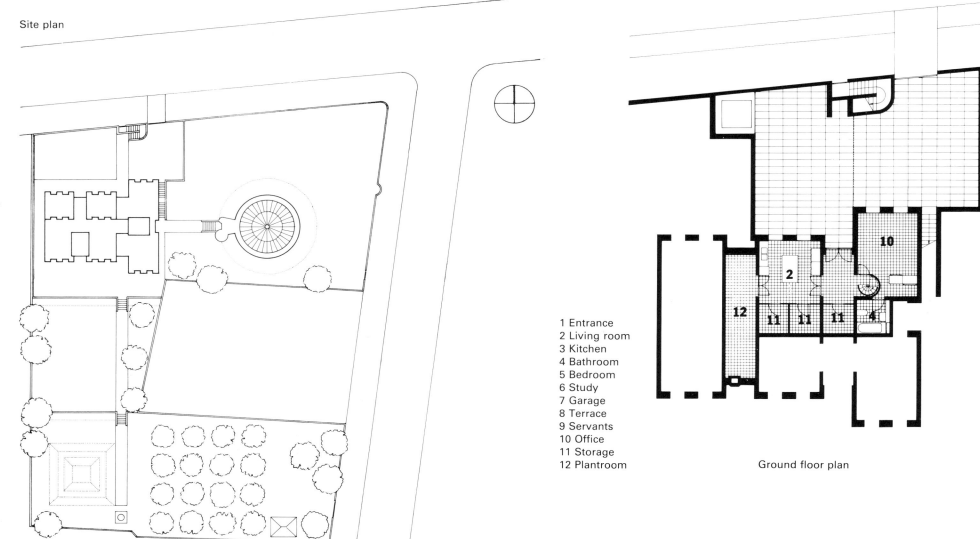

1 Entrance
2 Living room
3 Kitchen
4 Bathroom
5 Bedroom
6 Study
7 Garage
8 Terrace
9 Servants
10 Office
11 Storage
12 Plantroom

Ground floor plan

well made and designed, conceived as set-pieces within the overall order.

Furniture was specially designed for the house by Gowan and Chaim Schreiber. It consists of a system of plywood, bent into self-supporting forms and used in cupboards. The house was extended in 1967 by the addition of a circular swimming pool whose roof of glass is moulded to the surface, a pure sphere.

First floor plan

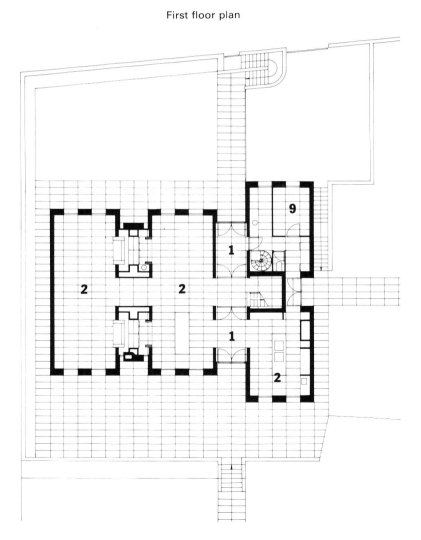

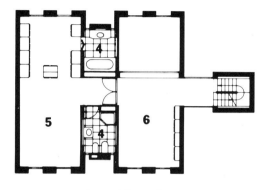

Second floor plan

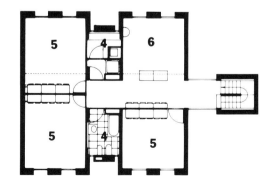

Third floor plan

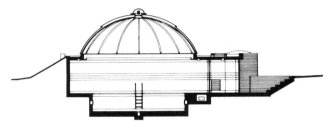

Swimming pool section

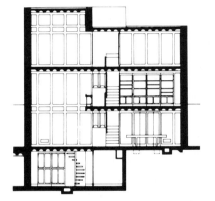

Section

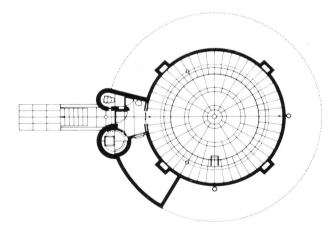

Swimming pool plan

Living room

Paul Rudolph: Town House

1966

While the construction plainly consists of a four-storey house at the front of the site and a 'mess' at the back, the spectacular innovation Rudolph made here was to roof over the space that would normally be garden so that it becomes a 27-foot-high living room.

The facade of the house is obscure brown glass framed in brown-painted steel. Only bedrooms 'face' the street. The view in the living room and the balcony bedroom at the rear of the site is either totally internal but lit from a skylight or to the three-storey greenhouse on the back wall of the lot.

In plan the house consists of a series of suites. The first, at ground and first floor levels, is kitchen dining area, the vast living room from which a staircase leads to changing rooms and bathrooms attached to the main double-height bedroom. On the floor above is an internal games room and bedroom with bathroom connected, and across the bridge attached to the party wall a further bedroom and bathroom. The roof has an almost self-contained apartment.

1 Entrance
2 Living room
3 Kitchen
4 Bathroom
5 Bedroom
6 Study
7 Garage
8 Terrace
9 Void

Drawn by Paul Barke

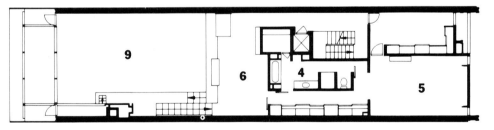

First floor plan

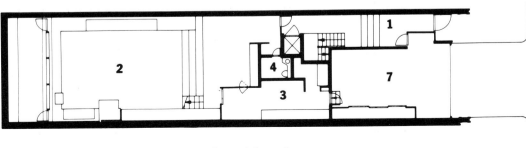

Ground floor plan

Rudolph's skill is clearly sectional manipulation. Within the section layers of vertical planes are contrasted with hanging plants or the two-storey-high bookcase. The original colour scheme, black slate, grey carpets, white walls, is programmatic – nature and light provide the colour.

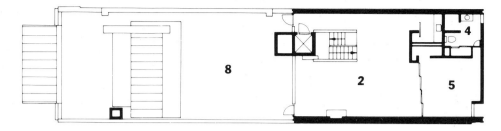

Third floor plan

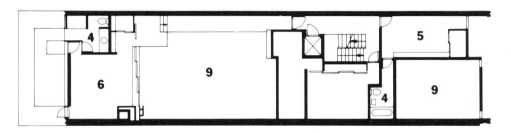

Second floor plan

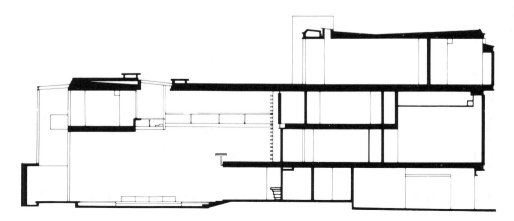

Section

Team 4: House at Creek Vean

The site faces south on a steep slope. A path from the higher level road divides the house. The path crosses a bridge and descends a magnificent Aalto-like flight of steps. Entrance to the house is into the two-storey living room space with kitchen beyond. From this, the lowest level, a passage beneath the flight of steps leads to a top-lit gallery, off which rooms splay towards the view. Each room can be divided from the gallery by sliding screens.

The materials of construction are concrete and concrete block, left fairfaced inside and out. Windows are of unframed toughened glass sliding in aluminium tracks. The long flat roof is covered with earth and planted with wild shrubs, ivy and grass.

The concept of the house is partway between a cave, and rooms attached to a forbidding wall. The complex section at the entry is the only architectural fanfare in an otherwise cool and ordered piece of work. Because of that, and the wide corridor, used as a gallery, it is hard to say how much of the house is used for circulation. This is the economical magic of the plan,

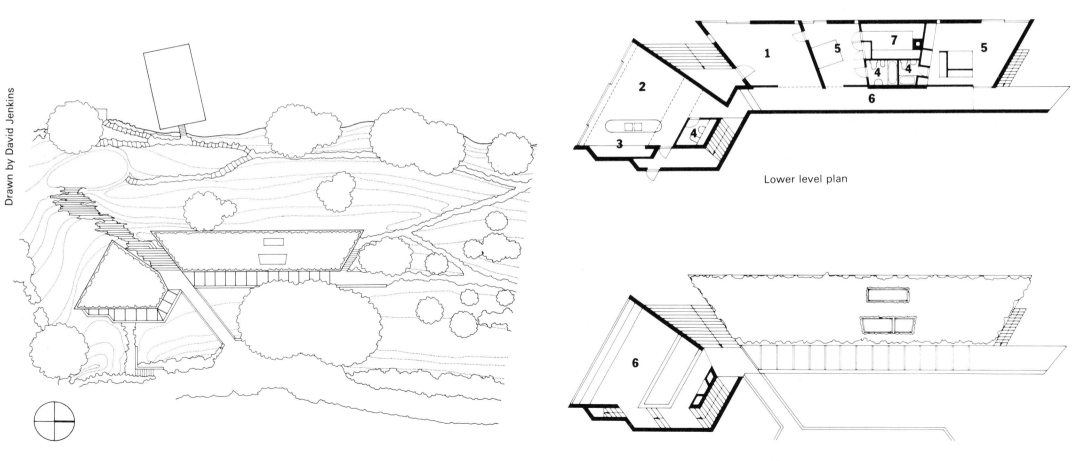

Drawn by David Jenkins

Site plan

Lower level plan

Upper level plan

64

and one problem which obsessed British architects in the sixties. Because the gallery can be read as the back wall of each room in the single-storey wing it is hard to read it as a corridor. Because of the tight and complex planning of the staircase and entry, with a smaller stair leading to a roof terrace over the two-storey wing, it is hard to measure any waste here.

This ingenuity contrasts beautifully with the ample and generous dimensions of all the main rooms.

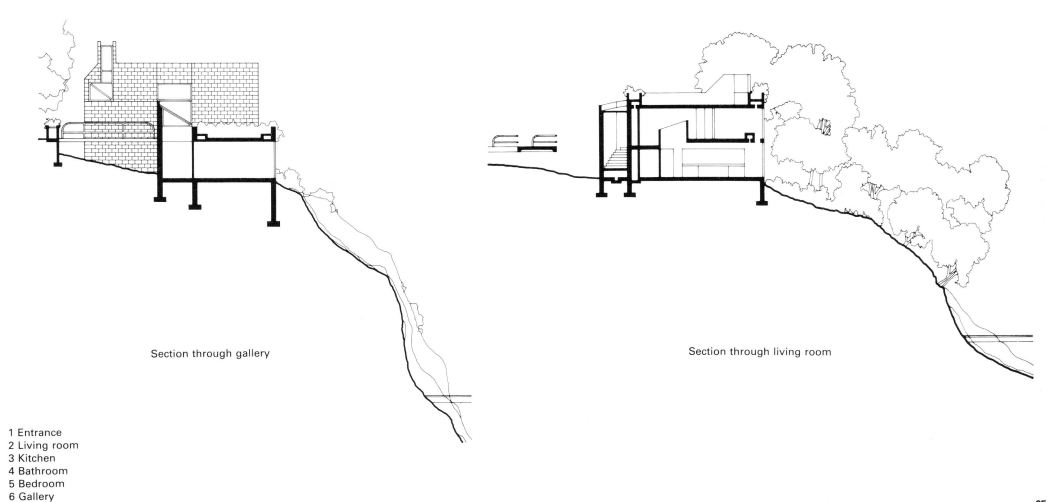

Section through gallery

Section through living room

1 Entrance
2 Living room
3 Kitchen
4 Bathroom
5 Bedroom
6 Gallery
7 Study

Team 4: Jaffé House
1966

This house resolves a classic design problem. With views to the north how can sunlight be brought into the house? The site also slopes at 1:8 to the north and is surrounded by suburban housing. The design solution is to place the house on a series of platforms stepping down the hill and to provide angled glazing between beams running on cross walls so that the view can be enjoyed, and the house flooded with light.

Three platforms drop down the slope, and the cross walls turn perpendicularly to the slope. At each of the three levels, however, the amount of accommodation changes. At the highest where the entrance is, to the left lies a study, to the right a conservatory and main bedroom. The next platform houses a dining space, kitchen and utility. The final platform has a living room, play room and children's bedrooms overlooked by the kitchen in the centre of gravity of the plan.

Despite the terracing the house is a grid of space which can be read from upmost to lowest platform, and equally across each platform. The

Drawn by Simon Colebrooke

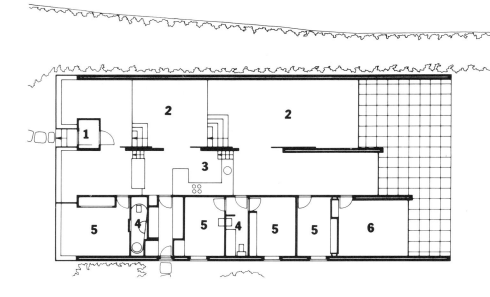

1 Entrance
2 Living room
3 Kitchen
4 Bathroom
5 Bedroom
6 Study

Plan
Ground floor plan

ingenuity of the plan depends upon this idea and the extremely simple constructional system. By English standards the result is a deep house plan in both dimensions. Without the device of the rooflights the kitchen would likely have become an external atrium. A series of sliding partitions enable the house to be understood as a space going between five cross walls with the bedrooms lined on the east side, or as a series of stepped tubes of spaces. Although conceived of as an extendable prototype, a group of these houses has never been constructed elsewhere.

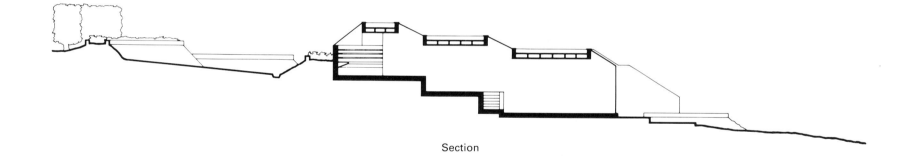

Section

Michael Graves: Hanselmann House

1967

There exists a tendency in twentieth-century houses for them to be approached from the north and entered through a blank facade. Graves' first house is entered from the south-east. Thus the view out to the south is through a glazed facade shielded by a second and blanker facade. The house's main elevation to the visitor thus has to perform two almost contra-dictory functions, which it achieves with a ser-ies of architectural devices deriving from a close study of modern precedent.

These devices are a contrast between frame and plane, between diagonal and curve, be-tween both and a bounding rectangle. But of greater importance is the conception of erosion by the architectural force upon a solid, frame or plane, The plane of entry, the south-east-facing facade, appears continuous from top to bottom and side to side but is eroded into strips, and a triangular balustrade for the staircase. A bal-cony protrudes to make a small overhang but a well-lit curved wall recedes above.

The section of the house has a double-height space over part of the living room and indicates

Drawn by Simon Colebrooke

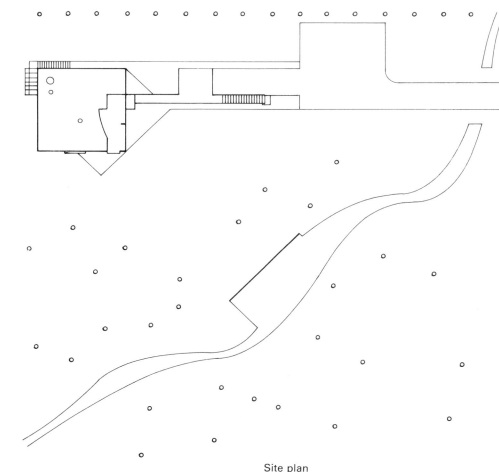

Site plan

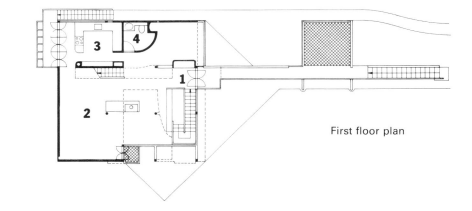

Ground level plan

First floor plan

the vertical zoning between children on the ground floor, the main living room above and overlooking that the master bedroom and study. The plan is a 3 x 3 grid with services located in the north corner, and opening up diagonally across to the south where the double-height space is guarded by the second-floor roof terrace.

In the original scheme a small pavilion was to have established the architectural themes of the house, reading from left to right, a steel frame, increasingly more solid, until it became a wall supported on a column. In the event only the staircase and walkway were constructed. Graves in this house revised the trend of his teachers, Gropius and Breuer, in seeking an American equivalent to European Modernism.

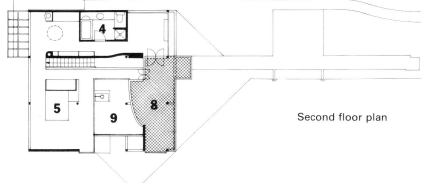

1 Entrance
2 Living room
3 Kitchen
4 Bathroom
5 Bedroom
6 Study
7 Garage
8 Terrace
9 Void over living room
10 Children's room

Second floor plan

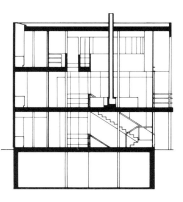

Section through living room

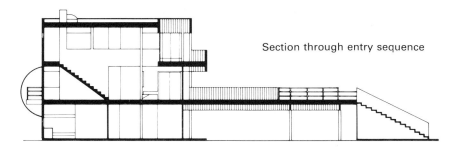

Section through entry sequence

Section through kitchen

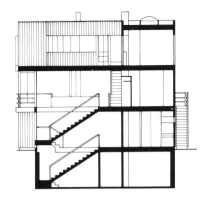

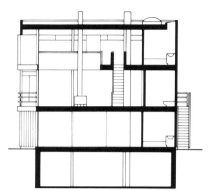

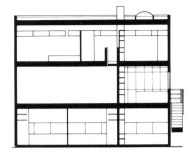

Section through staircase   Section through living room and terrace

Entry

Living room

John Howard: Mews House

The mews of London were first brought to popular attention in the film *Genevieve*, and were outshone there by the beauty of the late Kay Kendall. In that movie, the old stables of large houses were shown converted into garages with *pieds-à-terre* above. This small house for a couple, an artist and a publisher, was one of the first new houses in London in a mews,

but that is not its predominant distinction. The house is almost blank to the street, showing only two doors, one to the house, the other to the garage. From an entrance space, with a cloakroom to the left, steps rise to a dining lobby off which are a bathroom, the bedroom and a kitchen. A curved wall signals a staircase that rises to a living room that opens on to a

roof terrace, and off the living room lies a library, to the front and behind it a top-lit studio.

Throughout the house the advantage of such a free plan is used to give small enclosures with long internal vistas. The back-to-front dimension gives a clear line of sight from kitchen to the front door, and on the first floor diagonal

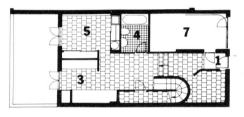

Ground floor plan

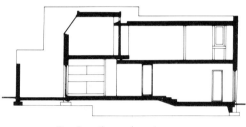

Section through entrance

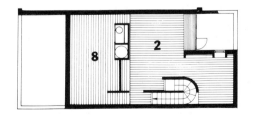

First floor plan

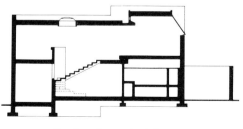

Section through staircase

Drawn by Alex Fergusson

views are emphasized. This sense of spaciousness is not simply scenographic. It is tied to the use of materials and construction. All cupboards and fittings are framed by walls, plastered where non-load bearing and painted brickwork where structural. This primary ordering device is continually matched against continuities of surface planes that bring to mind Dutch references, although hidden volumes carved out of wall planes dominate impressions of the interiors, as in the innovative kitchen.

The house has been lovingly maintained and remains one of the great interiors of the period, subtle, inventive and full of delight.

1 Entrance
2 Living room
3 Kitchen
4 Bathroom
5 Bedroom
6 Study
7 Garage
8 Studio

Street elevation

Frei Otto with Rob Krier: House and Studio at Warmbronn

1967

Two separate buildings sit on a south-facing 1:5 gradient. In the house two angled frames made from pine tree trunks provide the main support for timber beams supporting the greenhouse glazing. The base is concrete. Part of the 60° angle glazing to the south can be lifted by a cable winch to open the internal garden, with a small pool, to the sun.

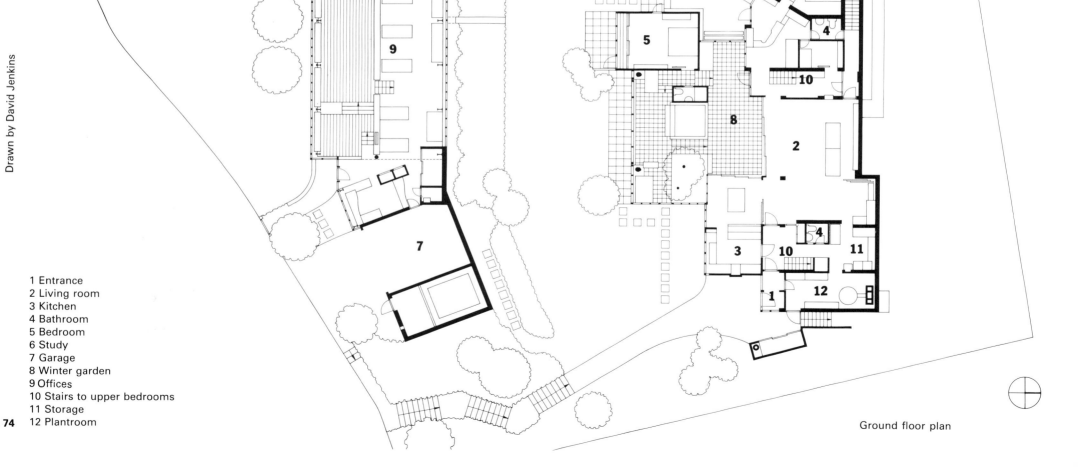

Drawn by David Jenkins

1 Entrance
2 Living room
3 Kitchen
4 Bathroom
5 Bedroom
6 Study
7 Garage
8 Winter garden
9 Offices
10 Stairs to upper bedrooms
11 Storage
12 Plantroom

Ground floor plan

The main accommodation of the house is a long strip set into the hillside. At lowest level this strip contains an array of workrooms and service space, although the kitchen is positioned in a separate box which protrudes from the main volume. At the higher level is a range of bedrooms, those for the children to the west, those for the parents to the east, each part accessed by a separate staircase. A guest room is placed at the south-west corner of the internal garden.

The studio building repeats the format of the main house but only its roof is visible from the house. It consists of a two-storey volume glazed to the south with a balcony. The garage is built into the slope to the east adjacent to this block. From there a staircase winds up the slope to provide the main entrance adjacent to the kitchen.

Considering its date, this house is one of the first to use an enclosing glass membrane as an energy-saving device. The accommodation is dealt with in a functional way with the internal garden uniting the diverse rooms. There is no obvious attempt at a functionalist aesthetic, but while pragmatism reigns the house has a strong feeling of adaptability because of the dominance of the central atrium.

As with all of Otto's work, there is a real experiment in construction and planning thought at work here. His laboratories at the University of Stuttgart have exactly the same drive.

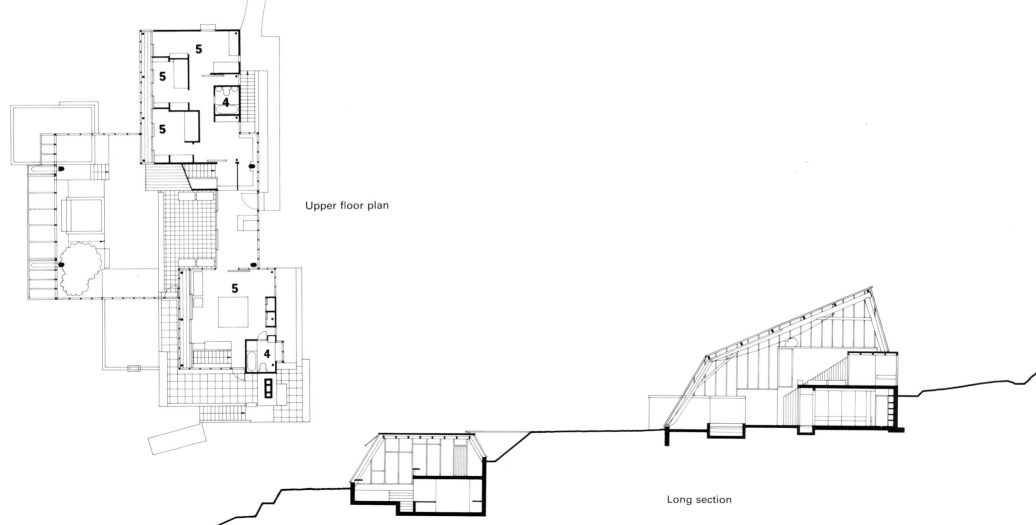

Upper floor plan

Long section

Robert Venturi and John Rauch: Trubeck and Wislocki Houses

Vincent Scully, in *The Shingle Style of Today* (Yale University Press, New Haven, 1971 p.36) spoke of these houses thus: 'With the Trubeck and Wislocki Houses we are in the presence of what modern architects have always said they most wanted: a true vernacular architecture – common, buildable, traditional in the deepest sense, and of piercing symbolic power'.

The exteriors have a family resemblance and so do the plans. Both ground floors are essentially one large room leading on to a broad porch overlooking the sea, with kitchens tucked into corners. The bedroom floor of the smaller house is a simple set of rooms. In the larger the spatial complexities around the stair-case are noteworthy, especially the division of the Palladian corridor to light both the stair-cases and the upmost floor's w.c.

The sections too show ingenuity, for while the exterior form may be borrowed from a vernacular, Venturi and Rauch have used every cubic inch of space within that form, so that the roof form is read within each bedroom.

Drawn by Luke Lowings

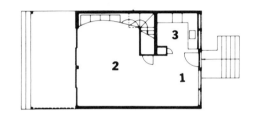

Ground floor plan

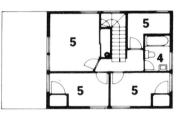

Upper floor plan

Elevation
Section

Trubeck house

1 Entrance
2 Living room
3 Kitchen
4 Bathroom
5 Bedroom

In the genre of holiday homes, the avid follower of middle class living patterns will be as familiar with the orange fridge by the sauna, as with the provencal pot next to the Magimix. These houses are almost elaborate tents for the use of city dwellers. The real purpose of vacationing, to be somewhere other but somewhere that belongs, receives from the architects a sophisticated reading. Apart from that, as architecture, these houses come close to fulfilling the rarely investigated dream of anonymity.

Ground floor plan

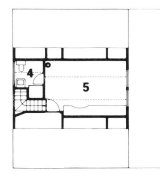

Upper floor plan

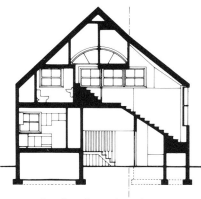

Section through staircase

First floor plan

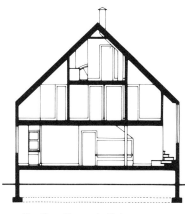

Section through living room

Wislocki house

1 Entrance
2 Living room
3 Kitchen
4 Bathroom
5 Bedroom
6 Porch

Alvaro Siza do Vieira: Cardoso House

1971

Portugal seems closer to an underdeveloped country than to Western Europe. Years of oppression finally ended in 1974. Modernism hardly had any foothold till then but since the change to democracy the figure of Alvaro Siza do Vieira has led a small renaissance. His concerns in architecture are not political, although all his public work stands forth against the begrimed critics as a beacon of clarity. In an introduction to his *oeuvre*, Alvari Siza do Vieira, *Poetic Profession*, Architectural Press, London, 1986, he wrote that his work 'is the outcome of participating in a process of cultural transformation which includes both construction and distinction'.

This house is a conversion of an extension to two small farm buildings. The extension is made out of plywood and timber in contrast to the rough stone of the existing buildings. A swimming pool has been added to the garden, which is kept as a vineyard.

The two existing buildings form an entry court. The upper floor of the smaller is made into two bedrooms and a bathroom. The larger

Drawn by Penny Gibson

1 Entrance
2 Living room
3 Kitchen
4 Bathroom
5 Bedroom

Ground floor plan

78

building in floor area has a kitchen carved out of the wing, which provides a further five bedrooms looking out on to, and shielded by, the vines. This wing is sunk slightly into the earth and surrounded by a stone wall. Above sill height all is timber and glass.

It would be inaccurate to read this scheme as a product of a conflict between twentieth-century rational planning and the existing vernacular. There is no conflict between the two rationales because the constructional techniques of each are in continual interplay. The real conflict is between the views and trees of the site and the buildings. This is Siza's achievement here: to subdue an additional architectural language to the pressure of the site.

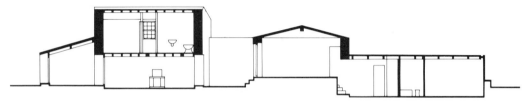

Section through entrance courtyard

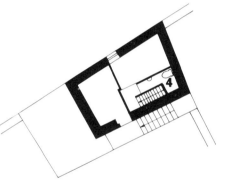

Upper floor plan

Section through garden

Lluis Clotet and Oscar Tusquets: Casa Vittoria

This rocky island, terraced for vines and olives, lies south of Sicily. The vernacular architecture, called 'damuso', of thick stone walls with shallow domical vaulting, is more African than Italian. No new buildings are permitted there, only extensions to existing structures.

Clotet and Tusquets have terraced their house into the hillside, and made the existing stucture

a bedroom and changing room. At this level they added a second bedroom and a bathroom. On the floor below is one large living space with kitchen to the east and built-in seating where the new building breaks away from the staircase. The occupants use the external steps built into the rock to go betwen the lower partly covered terrace to the upper one from

which they can then enter the spaces of the house.

From the sea the house, with its colonnades, appears to be a ruin. From the terraces the colonnades offer a sense of protection against the sea, and from the coast. The house itself becomes invisible behind these icons, as if it had always existed there as part of this

1 Entrance
2 Living room
3 Kitchen
4 Bathroom
5 Bedroom

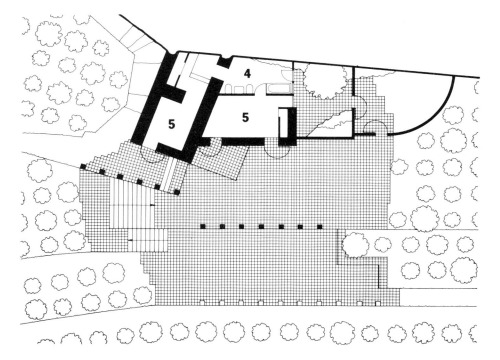

Upper level plan

landscape.

The power of the setting could have excited an architectural repsonse that wanted to erect a temple. Clotet and Tusquets resisted this for the more difficult and self-effacing solution whereby a single architectural element, a primitive colonnade, is juxtaposed with the stone-walled vernacular building. From such a lay-ering, the man-made aspect of the land-scape – its agricultural terracing – is raised to a strong and primitive dimension simply by sett-ing vertical columns against horizontal walls.

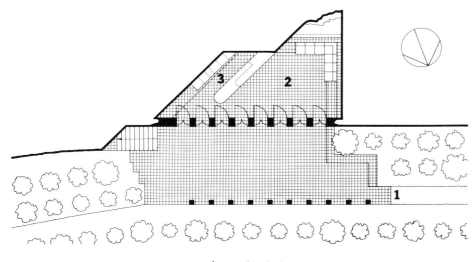

Lower level plan

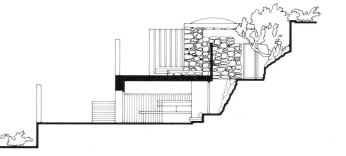

Section

Richard Meier: Shamberg Pavilion

From the first step on to the broadwalk leading to the front door it emerges how elegant and thoughtful this house is. Entry is made at the higher bedroom level, from which a staircase, modelled in plan on Le Corbusier's at the Pavilion Suisse, gives a grand almost Hollywood entrance to the living area. The entry wall is a thick zone in plan of servant rooms, which acts as a barrier to enhance entry as a dramatic event, piercing a wall to receive the magnificent view. Then it acts inside the house as a backdrop to the architectural events of cranked staircase, structural frame, free-standing fireplace and chimney and beyond that the single-storey dining room with bedroom and terrace above.

These elements are juxtaposed in space as sculptural pieces flooded with light and not compacted. The effect of this is to give great weight to the choice and disposition of furniture. Clearly only pieces equal to the architecture could be used, as indeed the architecture has become fixed furniture.

This is not to belittle the ingenuity with

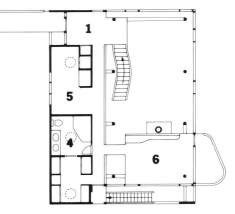

Upper level plan

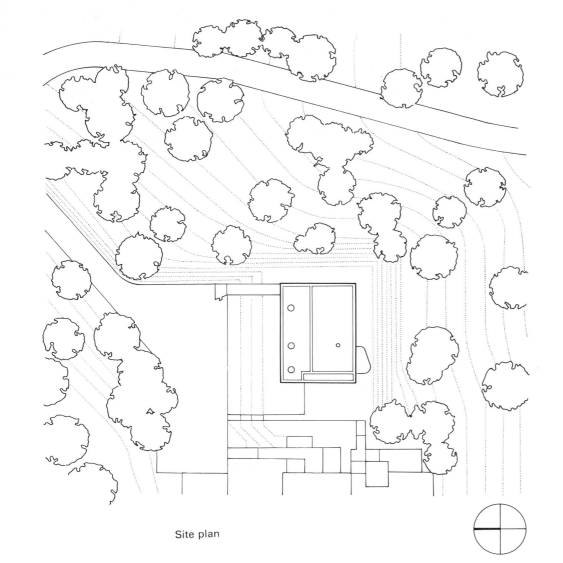

Site plan

1 Entrance
2 Living room
3 Kitchen
4 Bathroom
5 Bedroom
6 Study

Drawn by Paul Barke

which Meier studies his chosen antecedent, both adapting that work to an American context and advancing beyond the fine points. There are no opaque walls here, nor any unsystematic structural tricks, as at the Villa Savoie. Instead the games of inside/outside – the balcony and the two staircases – are made to seem relaxed. The roof appears not to be intended as a terrace.

South elevation

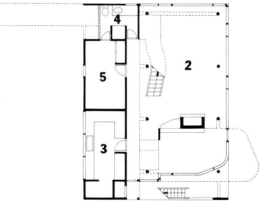

Lower level plan

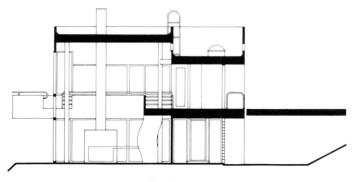

Section

Frank Westergaard: House at Herning

1973

The plan of this house can be read in two ways. Firstly as a courtyard house, secondly as an L-shaped house with a pavilion. The latter interpretation becomes stronger if the plan is seen to be a row of bedrooms to the north from which two kinds of living room are attached, one, the smaller, which is separated as a pavilion, and has only low level windows, a room,

the other, an open plan space.

This ambiguity suggests the depth of functional thought which has contributed to the scheme. The larger living room is to some extent a barn kitchen with a gallery, not completely extended by the owners. Inside the barn is a low brick wall surrounding an ingle-nook around the fireplace. This structure is posi-

tioned to divide the space into a set of open but discrete spaces, whose individual scale is marked by the window openings.

Entrance is adjacent to the kitchen; from that facade the severe mode of the design is made plain. Openings in the brick walls have thermopane windows set in a steel frame, and made to seem slightly larger by a frame of

1 Entrance
2 Living room
3 Kitchen
4 Bathroom
5 Bedroom
6 Study

Drawn by Alex Fergusson

Ground floor plan

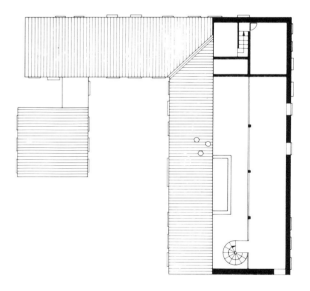

Gallery/roof plan

bricks disengaged by a vertical joint from the wall proper. These windows are not openable. All openings in that sense have timber-panelled doors.

From the inside the windows do not seem to exist, because their frame is fixed to the exterior. From the outside they appear as a series of mirrors to the surroundings. The brickwork dominates, and behaves on the exterior like the wall of an art gallery. This severity on the outside is a positive force on the inside, where the rooms by virtue of the construction of the windows seem almost relics of a past. It is this phenomenon which makes the house an extraordinary experiment, neither vernacular nor historicist.

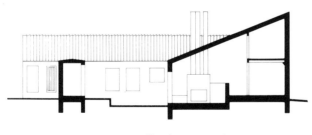

Section

Rob Krier: House, Luxembourg

Krier has explained in a series of diagrams how the house is assembled from four elements, a cube, a plane, either vertical or horizonal, a column, and a grid-like transparent lattice, a series, that is, that moves from solid geometry to transparency. In the house itself no element is present in totality: the cube has a corner cut out, the column is not free standing, the lattice is folded into a complex form and the planes are invisible.

The listing of elements, parallel to that of Le Corbusier, is not the only homage paid. The house, while not on pilotis, and lacking an interior double-height volume, has a stratified section with garage and service rooms in the basement, an open-plan living/dining room with kitchen on the first floor, three bedrooms on the second floor and a studio and roof terrace on the top floor.

The more recent housing in West Berlin by Krier is obsessive about rooms. In this earlier house softer forms are articulated against the fragmented elements. The staircase protrudes through one wall, and a sculpture is set by the

Basement plan

First floor plan

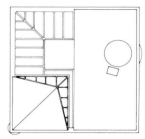

Roof plan

Ground floor plan

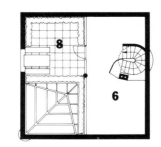

Second floor plan

Section

terrace. The bedroom floor too shows a kind of planning more akin to Erskine than the rationalism associated with Krier's name.

This comment underlines the essential humanism of Rob Krier's approach to architecture. The house is a prototype if seen as an abstraction of shelter, but it is warmed through with a concern for use and an acute perception of interior space. To that extent, and to the extent that it has personal qualities, it is hardly prototypical. Moreover, the forms inside and out have little to do with the villa from which the brief derives. In short, it is an invention.

Staircase wall

Corner elevation

1 Entrance
2 Living room
3 Kitchen
4 Bathroom
5 Bedroom
6 Study
7 Garage
8 Terrace

Robert A.M. Stern: Town House

1974

The ground floor of this design is given over to another use. The house proper therefore begins on the piano nobile, with deep living floor typical of brownstones. But this floor is three half-levels around a three-storey square lightwell and it is protected from the circulatory corridor by a sinuous wall. The kitchen is to the rear. The second half-level is over the entrance and the third half-level is a full floor above the dining space. At the rear are two bedrooms with a further one borrowing light from an adjacent lightwell. The top floor is the main bedroom with all associated rooms no civilised rich New Yorker could live without. A roof terrace/garden divides this from two more bedrooms. Stern is the most practised domestic planner in America. The spaces within his houses flow effortlessly, whatever architectural style he plays with. This house is no exception but is one of his most sophisticated exercises.

Three main architectural devices are employed to give a grand scale to the house. The first is the sinuous wall first seen on entry at the piano nobile. This is a wall of ranging

Drawn by David Jenkins

Basement floor plan

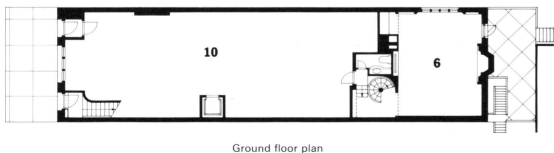

Ground floor plan

1 Entrance
2 Living room
3 Kitchen
4 Bathroom
5 Bedroom
6 Study
7 Garage
8 Terrace
9 Servants
10 Office
11 Storage
12 Plantroom

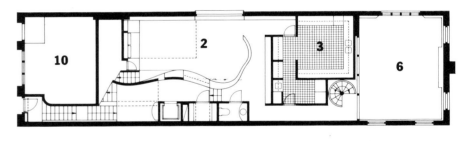

First floor plan

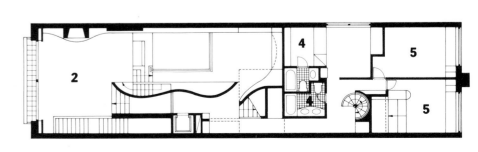

Second floor plan

thickness used on the living side as a piece of furniture, as a balustrade repeated in the ceiling, as a lit gash and engaging all of the semi-public spaces.

The second device is the three-storey light-well which visually relates the owner's bedroom to the living room, but, most important, provides vertical dimension to an essentially horizontally stratified space. The third device is the bulging wall of the fireplace. This intrudes in the most narrow dimension of the plan – the sitting room in front of the big street window. From it horizontal inset stripes of yellow visually connect to other parts.

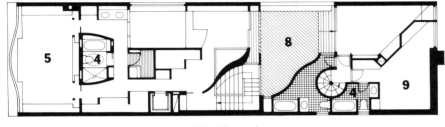

Third floor plan

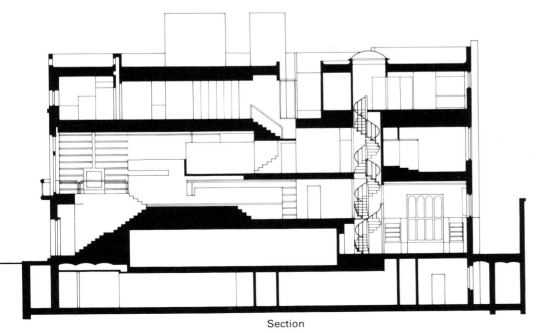

Section

Street elevation

William Turnbull: Zimmerman House

The site is a low ridge of land, the flood plain of the Potomac river. The house was designed for a couple and their three children. The formal solution offered to the clients' diverging requirements, on the one hand for orderly rooms and controlled light, on the other for a free flow of space and lots of sun, was to set up a cubical framework of trellis, within which rooms are disposed according to functional requirements. The trellis/frame also hides the almost Loosian build-up of volumes and provides acres of outdoor terraced space. At strategic points for view the trellis is pierced by framed 'windows'.

The separation of exterior form from interior volumes is at its most extreme in this building. Turnbull used the standard American timber-frame technique to maximum effect to produce the double-layered facade. But it is not simply disorder. Two systems of circulation control the plan. On the outside, between the trellis and the actual walls of the rooms, is a series of terraces which are related so that the walk up them is almost like a ('short') promenade up a ziggurat. Then inside the house a top-lit stair-

Drawn by David Jenkins

Basement floor plan

1 Entrance
2 Living room
3 Kitchen
4 Bathroom
5 Bedroom
6 Study

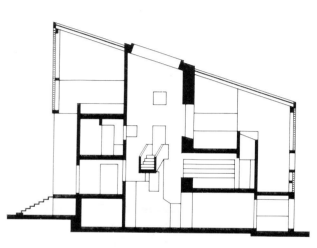

Section

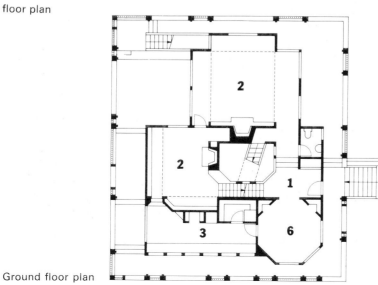

Ground floor plan

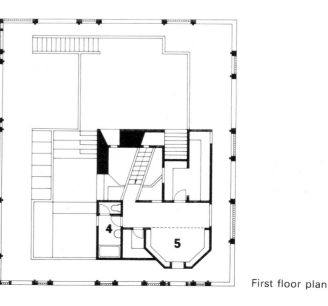

First floor plan

case hall forms the centre quasi-atrium space of the house.

This elegant solution is achieved by allowing what would normally have been understood as *poche* spaces to have an existence of their own.

Entrance elevation

Peter Eisenman: House VI

1976

Eisenman's career, as teacher, writer, theorist and latterly architect, speaks of a cultural schizophrenia. The split is between a desire for an almost automatic architecture, devoid of function, user or expression, but one generated from those conceptual analyses of form he found in his research on Terragni on the one hand, and a colossal ego on the other. The beauty of the beast is in two houses, the first House II of 1969, and this one of six years later.

Two planes intersect a cube which reverberates between frame and solid as a result. William Gass, reviewing the house in *Progressive Architecture*, was delighted by the play of light and shade, and horrified by the kitchen sink, which was 'like a kiss in the middle of a cough'.

Eisenman would like to void the concept 'house' of any historical connotation. In line with this the rooms are more or less undesignated. But a simple suburban typology of space intervenes and the living rooms are on the ground floor, the bedrooms up above. The schizophrenia of Eisenman's incessant theore-

Ground floor plan

First floor plan

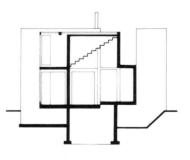

Section

Section

1 Entrance
2 Living room
3 Kitchen
4 Bathroom
5 Bedroom

tical justification versus the pragmatics of construction, and even a simple architectural desire to build, is easily diagnosed, a posteriori. Yet the idea of what can be done in tectonic, if not architectural, forms with the limits of possibility of existence have remarkably been charted in this pavilion, demonstrating both architects' ingenuity and clients' ingenuousness.

Exterior view

Living room

Fabio Reinhardt and Bruno Reichlin: Casa Tonino

The Ticino, the smallest canton of Switzerland, is linked by language to Italy. Whereas elsewhere in that country a visitor searches in vain for good recent work, this canton has enough new work to make it, along with Spain, the place where the dreams of a twentieth-century architecture have not become nightmares.

Since the exhibition, 'Tendenza', many Ticinese architects who were first exhibited there have developed a strong and individual set of concerns. The climate demands sturdy building, the culture is European, and the forms are platonic. Reinhardt and Reichlin's house looks south to Vicenza, and obviously to the Villa Rotonda. But that only speaks of the tartan grid and the pyramidal composition, nearly equal on all four sides. That side facing the valley has an arch detached from the house, purposeless except as a symbol, a form awaiting interpretation and inscription.

Within a four-columned hall rises almost independently of the roof form. Each corner bay, in varying configurations, contains a room (a study or bedroom). On the first floor a long

Drawn by Simon Colebrooke

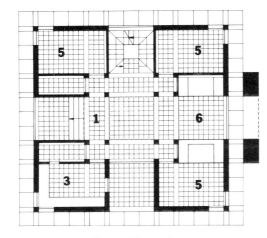

Ground floor plan

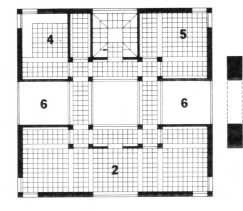

First floor plan

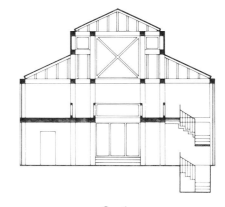

Section

1. Entrance
2. Living room
3. Kitchen
4. Bathroom
5. Bedroom
6. Void

room stretches across the plan. It is reached by a staircase Palladio would have not had to locate anywhere except in the *poche*. This upper floor breathes upwards.

Thereby the house is not pastiche, but an attempt at invention within a difficult language spoken in hard times. The architects have written, 'Now the performances are family ones: exhibitions, congresses, books and magazines: both the performers and the audience are architects. Many projects are sentenced to the limbo of paper. It cannot last'.

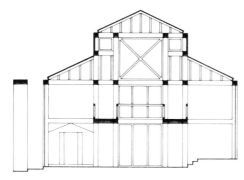

Section through voids

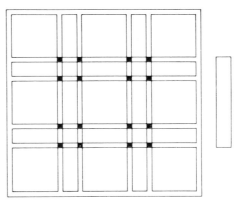

Roof plan

Elevation to valley

Taller d'Arquitectura: House at Montras

This scheme consists of six separate houses grouped to mirror the structure of the family. The grandparents wanted a holiday home set among orchards behind the Costa Brava where their children and their grandchildren could assemble. They, the grandparents, have a three-storey L-shaped house with a monumental entrance set diagonally to the swimming pool. Across the pool lies a communal dining room for everyone and behind this sit five brick towers for the children and their children. These towers are based on a volume 3 x 6 x 6 metres which has two levels and is really a sort of motel maisonette. One tower, adjacent to the dining room, contains the kitchen and above that is a spare bedroom.

The ideal of family life has been given a form in this scheme, which respects to some extent the identity of the members. Moreover, the scale, although monumentally constructed out of dark blue brick, lacks the megalomania with which this office is associated. At the same time a rigorous geometry pervades the layout, and this comes to the fore most in the outdoor

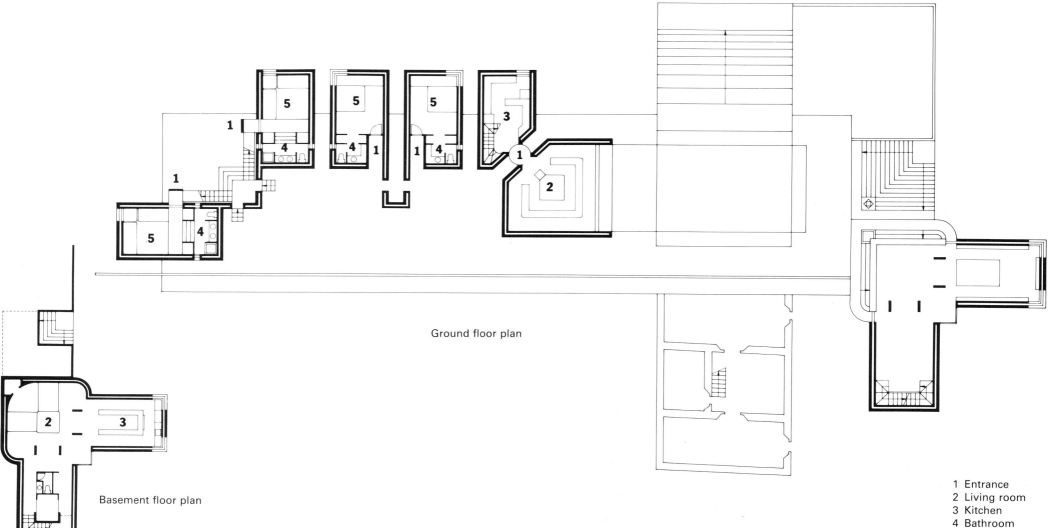

Ground floor plan

Basement floor plan

Drawn by David Jenkins

1 Entrance
2 Living room
3 Kitchen
4 Bathroom
5 Bedroom

96

spaces where the brickwork, the tower/
sentinels and the open but formal plan of the
grandparents' house blend together to evoke a
family structured and ritualized, but at play.

First floor plan

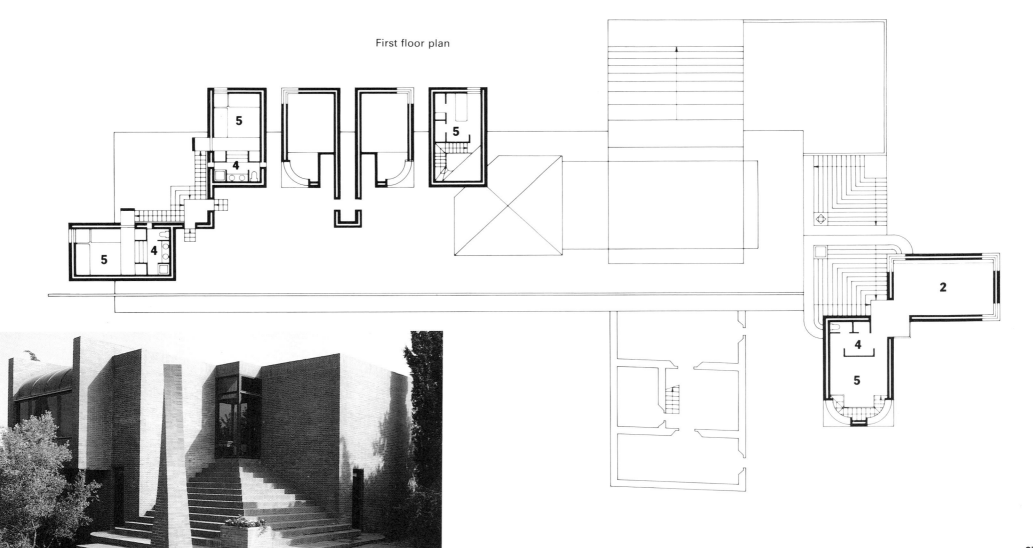

Corner entrance

Tadao Ando: Horiuchi House

1978

In many countries bordering the Pacific basin there has been a move among architects to seek national identity. The reasons for this are mostly economic, the domination of the international capital and the homogenization of place which necessarily results. Against these factors the Australians, Malays and Californians have all struggled to establish what has not heretofore needed to exist, a sense in architecture of national identity. Japanese architecture in general seems to have avoided this impasse. Perhaps because Japanese architects, the children of *the* post-war boom economy have no sense of inferiority to the West, and are confident in their position within Japanese society as givers of form.

This certainly appears true of Ando. This house is a universal object, neither locked into its site nor into local materials in a way westerners would immediately understand. What we can grasp is the forcefulness of the volume and its spaces, and above that of the strength of the client in allowing the architect space to experiment.

Drawn by David Jenkins

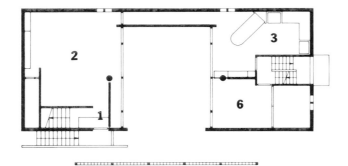

First floor plan

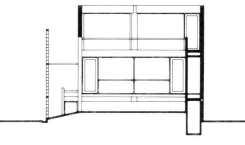

Section

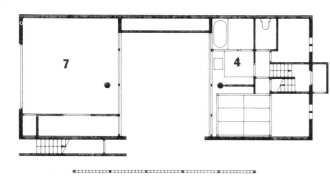

Ground floor plan

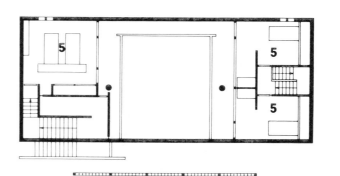

Second floor plan

This liberty, rarely seen now, is grasped by Ando particularly in the disposition of the two zones. Access to the farthest zone is across a corridor, thus making the house an almost entirely self-contained entity. The promenade through is dominated by concrete bounding walls; the views are limited either to the internal courtyard, which is nearly an exact mirror image, or to the sky.

In this house there is no transition between the public space of the street and the private enclosed world of the house.

1 Entrance
2 Living room
3 Kitchen
4 Bathroom
5 Bedroom
6 Study
7 Garage

Living room

Screen to street

Frank Gehry: Own House

Strictly speaking this is not a new house but a refurbishment and extension of an existing typical Californian house. What Gehry has achieved though is a dramatic and evocative totality in which the new and the existing unite in a particular experiment. The tradition of extending houses is twofold: either to add more of the same or to juxtapose new with old.

Gehry's experiment is to transform the typical house by wrapping a new house around it, and to contrast both new and existing continuously.

The materials used are both real and virtual. The material that is least real, most virtual, is the chain-link fence, hardly admitted previously to the list of things architecture can be made of.

In his use of such materials, Gehry returns to the problem of using American materials, namely wood, sheet rock, chain-link fencing, etc. to produce a vernacular, in this case one local to Southern California.

From his work and his interests in this problem has sprung the so-called new wave of California architects. The first modern wave

Drawn by Alex Fergusson

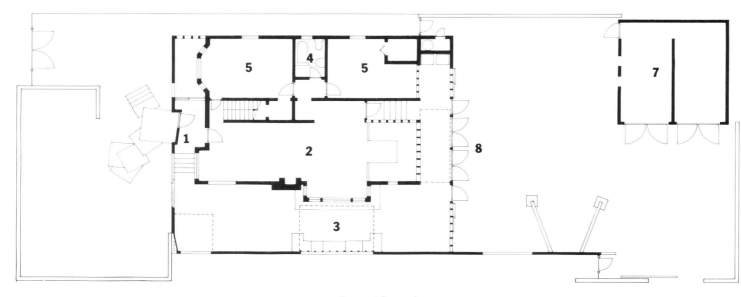

Ground floor plan

1 Entrance
2 Living room
3 Kitchen
4 Bathroom
5 Bedroom
6 Study
7 Garage
8 Terrace

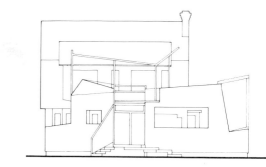

Entrance elevation

learnt from the Harvard Europeans and from Neutra and Schindler. This, the second wave, lacks the cultural inferiority complex and is at ease with southern California as it is. What experiments like this depend on are clear existing forms against which surprise variations can be played. The second wave explores both typologies, and is perhaps the first architecture to spring from a developed suburban context.

Exterior

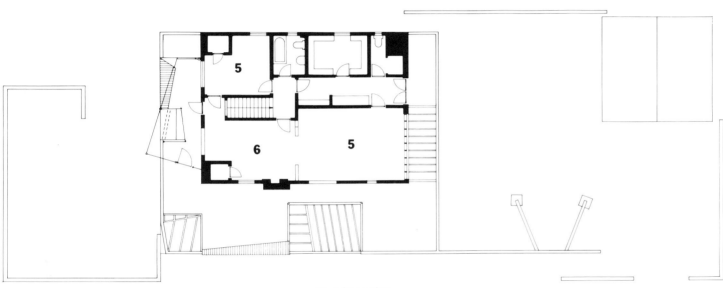

First floor plan

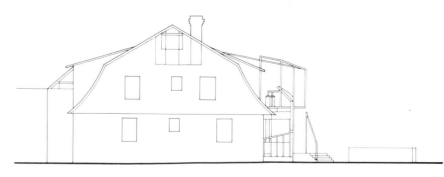

Flank elevation

Marco Zanuso: House on Lake Como

Zanuso is the designer of many icons of the new Italian Domestic Landscape, among which the black cube television, sadly no longer in production, was an admirable minimal industrial design. His work as an architect is less well known, although a factory in Buenos Aires (1959) displayed a remarkable integration of services and structure, as well as being easily extendable.

Roberto Guiducci, writing in *Casabella* 229, attributes a will to use 'existing materials as a sign of the times, so that everyone should speak a true idiom and not invent a personal and incommunicable language'. This informs the house on Lake Como, a simple L-shaped plan with every service in the right place and a quiet pleasure in the materials. Nothing is overstated, nor is the house used as the occasion for polemic. This is a strand of Modernism Italy has almost lost.

Ground floor plan

1 Entrance
2 Living room
3 Kitchen
4 Bathroom
5 Bedroom
6 Study

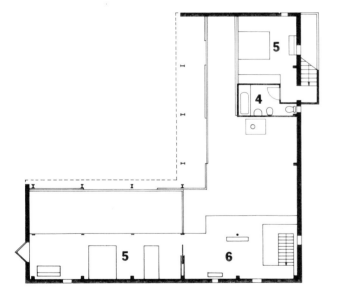

First floor plan

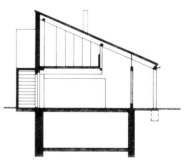

Section

Andrew Batey and Mark Mack: Kirlin House

1979

Batey was trained in the History of Art at Oxford and then read architecture at Cornell. He has worked for Norman Foster and Luis Barragán. Mack was trained in Graz and Vienna and has worked for Emilio Ambasz. From these backgrounds it is no surprise that their buildings are learned, involved with conceptions of type, and strongly influenced by a purity of construction that is hardly American. In the Anti-Villa, an earlier project in the Napa Valley, the house is cut into the hillside, and constructed of concrete blocks; glazing is steel sash windows. Entrance is down a staircase through a zone of service rooms. A long corridor runs between these rooms, which have specific designations, and a set of four other rooms which do not. The latter open on to a trellis-covered terrace. The corridor is top lit and from it the living spaces borrow light.

The Kirlin House, by contrast, has an ample plan with a central living space on either side of which are two wings. The whole is enclosed by high walls that are like adobe construction. Two courtyards complete the rectangle in plan,

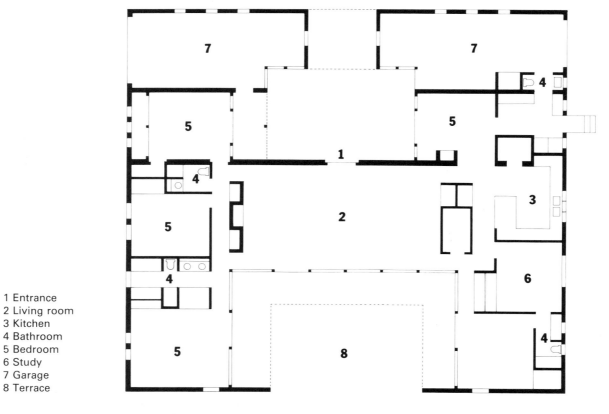

1 Entrance
2 Living room
3 Kitchen
4 Bathroom
5 Bedroom
6 Study
7 Garage
8 Terrace

Ground floor plan

Drawn by Alex Fergusson

the north-facing being the entry court, the south-facing opening more gently on to vineyards.

The plan consists of three elements: firstly, the thick external wall which is repeated in the entry face of the north court. Secondly, the frame and glass enclosure of the courtyards, an element which gives light to most rooms.

Thirdly, all divisions between rooms, more built-in closets, services and furniture than walls.

This degree of rationalization is hardly associated with the California new wave. It is clearly European in derivation, but American in form. If that aspect is subverted by a deliberate simplicity of design, the result is certainly more histo-

ricist than anything else. But historicist in the sense of the history of the invasion by Europe of America, when the Spanish imposed a planning typology wherever they settled.

Living room

Courtyard

Mario Botta: House at Ligornetto

1979

Most of Botta's houses work with the site as an idealized concept. The house at Riva San Vitale is a tower, accessible apparently only from the highest level. A perfectly useful road also approaches it at the lowest floor of the tower. At Ligornetto the site is conceptualized by Botta as if it were the edge of the village. From afar it is a (perfectly formed) slice of a striped wall.

But this handy conceit enables Botta to explore a long thin three-storey volume as if it could receive light only from above or from a hole punched into its centre of gravity.

The plan contains garaging, laundry and store rooms at ground floor level, living rooms and children's bedrooms at first floor and a study and master bedroom on the third. Despite the

continuity of the striped concrete block wall the house is composed in plan of two equal-sized parts, where the cut between the two, facing south-west, contains two overstepping terraces. The two major rooms of the house, the living room and parents' bedroom, are treated as termini. The living room has a large semi-circular arched fireplace, top lit through a gash

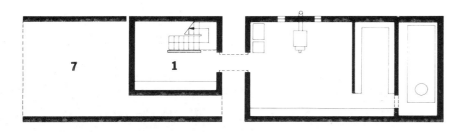

Ground floor plan

Second floor plan

First floor plan

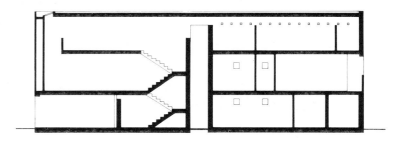

Section through staircase

in the section that relates that room to the study above, while the bedroom has a bed axially positioned to a wall separated from the enclosing structure, behind which are the his-and-hers changing spaces.

The hierarchy evident in the plan has a kind of freezing charm, and almost anaesthetized glamour. The house is designed to affect the way people live through the patterns of use it offers but also through its almost sacred imagery.

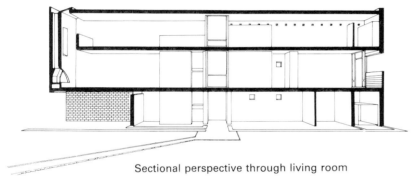

Sectional perspective through living room

Road elevation

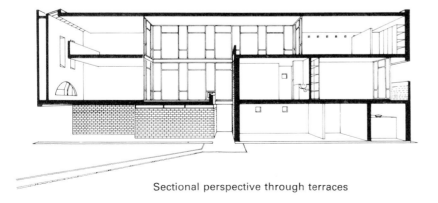

Sectional perspective through terraces

1 Entrance
2 Living room
3 Kitchen
4 Bathroom
5 Bedroom
6 Study
7 Garage
8 Terrace

Jeronimo Junquera and Estanislao Peréz Pita: House at Santander

1984

Set above a subsidiary bay of the great Biscay port of Santander, this vacation house is a remarkable variation on the theme of a house within a house. In this case the house accommodation is held in a square, along two sides of which are a double-height conservatory. The landward side has a vestigial cornice on the top of the concrete frame filled in with glass. The house itself has openings into this conservatory which are closed when the house is left by steel roller shutters. The floor of the conservatory is simply wooden planks suspended over the ground so that jasmine, orange trees and other plants have begun to invade the space.

The house is a retreat, built by the architect for his wife and two children. As a wall to the entry and frame to the view it sits within a northern Spanish tradition of building which would be out of place in any other part of the country. The climate of Santander is not harsh, but prone to rain. The part of the vacation which is an essential complement to this house is the boat. In good weather the family take to it.

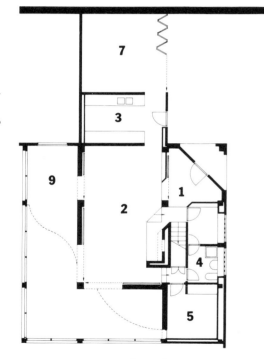

Drawn by Luke Lowings

Ground floor plan

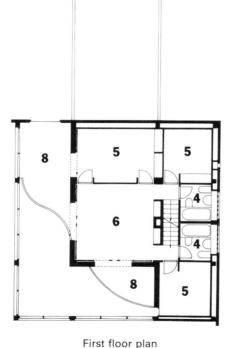

First floor plan

1 Entrance
2 Living room
3 Kitchen
4 Bathroom
5 Bedroom
6 Study
7 Garage
8 Terrace
9 Conservatory

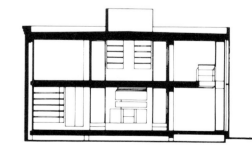

Section

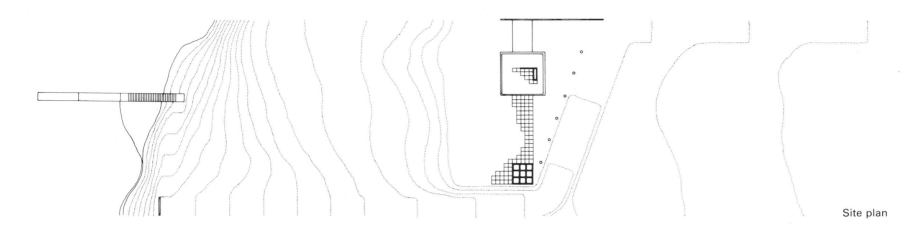

Site plan

Conservatory

Exterior

Glen Murcutt: House at Bingie Point

1985

When the whole conceptual apparatus of Modernism appears untenable, and at exactly the moment when any notion of form deriving from constructions seemed just a woolly-minded nostalgia, the buildings of Glenn Murcutt were published. This makes him something of an architectural hero, operating a one-man, one-job-at-a-time practice, and talking, like Eero Saarinen, about smelling the site.

Whereas Californians used material of the ghetto for symbolic purposes, Murcutt employs corrugated iron as a material, as Utzon used concrete in the Sydney Opera House, still waiting for forms to be developed from inside the material's potential.

The house is severe, ritualized in plan; outside it's a shack, but a shack that is turned to high-frequency vibrations, from the world of technology as much as from the world proper.

He has written: 'Before an architecture of consequence can be established, the genius of the landscape must be appreciated and absorbed so that the place is understood. To this end, I have ventured outside the cities and

End view

Site plan

Living room

towns and into the land which has been minimally changed. That is the only way I can find a friendship with landscape, to sense the wind, rain, heat and cold, the smells and colours, the flora and the horizontality, the light and the vastness which make up such a tough but supremely delicate land.'

1 Entrance
2 Living room
3 Kitchen
4 Bathroom
5 Bedroom
6 Study
7 Garage
8 Terrace

North–sun facing–elevation

Section

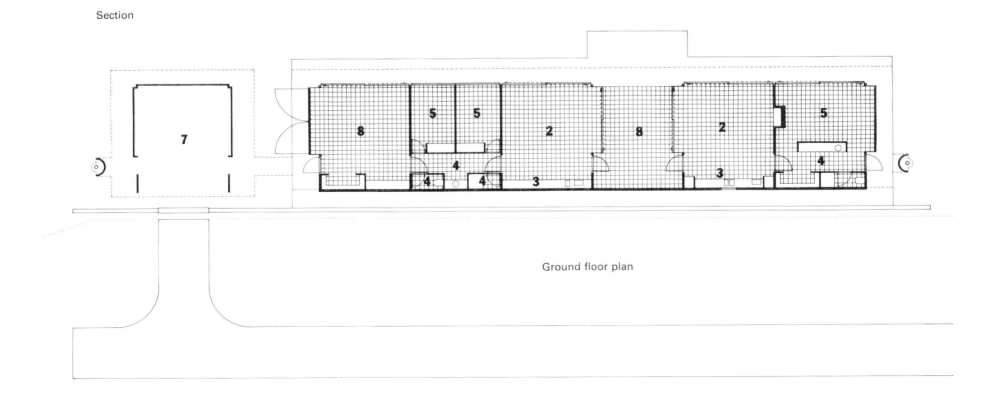

Ground floor plan

Eldred Evans and David Shalev: House at Twickenham

The site lies in a mews behind a fine early Georgian terrace. There are only views into the garden and so the architects have created a plan which at first-floor level fragments into a Z-shape to permit light to enter a deep ground-floor plan.

From the news one enters through a low porch into a tall space flooded with light. From here down three steps a low-ceilinged living room is reached, to the left of which angled glazing lights the northern wall. A semi-circular bay sits on the garden side. Thus the spatial sequence from entry to garden alternates between dark and light.

The added benefit of the disposition of the upper floor is that two distinct and separate bedrooms are constructed, the smaller room looking on to the mews but with a balcony internal to the light-flooded hall, and the larger bedroom enjoying a terrace on top of the semi-circular bay window.

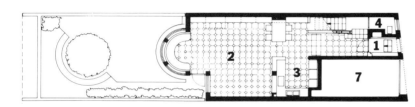

Ground floor plan

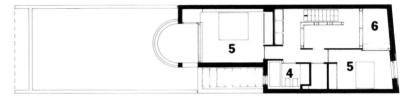

First floor plan

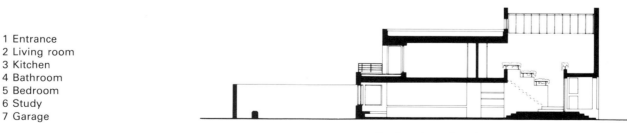

Section through staicase

1 Entrance
2 Living room
3 Kitchen
4 Bathroom
5 Bedroom
6 Study
7 Garage

Drawn by David Jenkins

Section

Elevation

Section

Elevation

113

Maggie Edmond and Peter Corrigan: Athan House

1989

Corrigan was one of the first intelligent commentators on Venturi, whose influence on his work was at first marked and now clearly diminishing. This design overlays two themes but fractures both. The first theme appears in plan as two vertical planes against which circulation runs, meeting at the hinge of the main entrance. The second theme is the sectional intersection of roof or ground and external wall which provides a range of bay windows, overhangs and terraces.

The plan inside consists of two routes, off one of which lie bedrooms and off the other a suite of interconnecting rooms leading from dining room to kitchen to living room to study. This last suite externally is read as two compositions by virtue of terraces attaching to the slope themselves, decorated with furniture-like canopies and gates.

The scheme in its finished state is highly coloured, thus setting a further thematic layering over the design, imperceptible in drawings. While every room looks out on to a beautiful site, the internal triangular court, containing

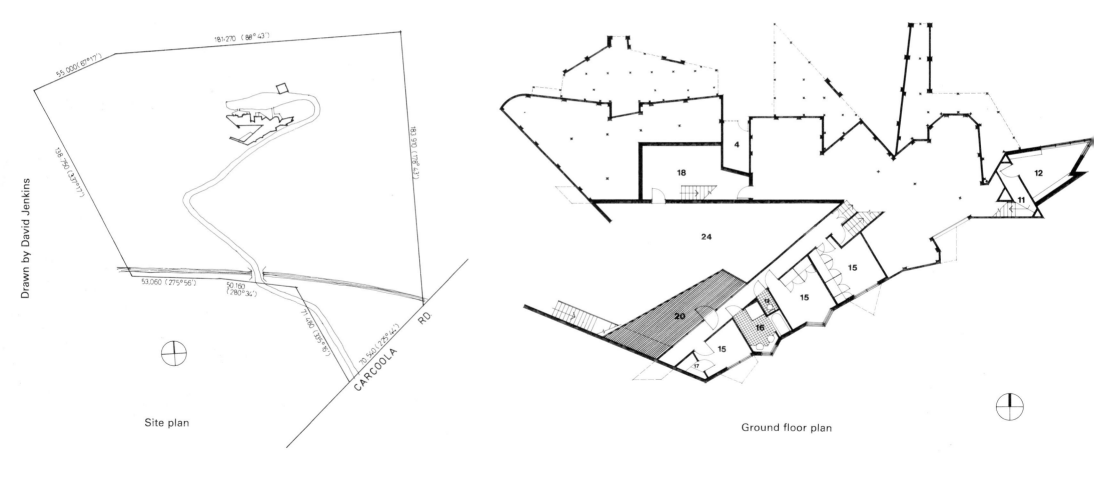

Drawn by David Jenkins

Site plan

Ground floor plan

the winter gardens, offers an almost urban oasis.

1 Studio
2 Laundry
3 Living Room
4 Aviary
5 Kitchen
6 Greenhouse Ferner
7 Dining Room
8 Cloak Room
9 Entry Foyer
10 Parlor
11 Stairwell
12 Library
13 Toilet
14 Ensuite
15 Bedroom
16 Bathroom
17 Storage
18 Cellar
19 Balcony
20 Decking
21 Breakfast Seat
22 Artist's Seat
23 Entry Bridge
24 Winter Garden

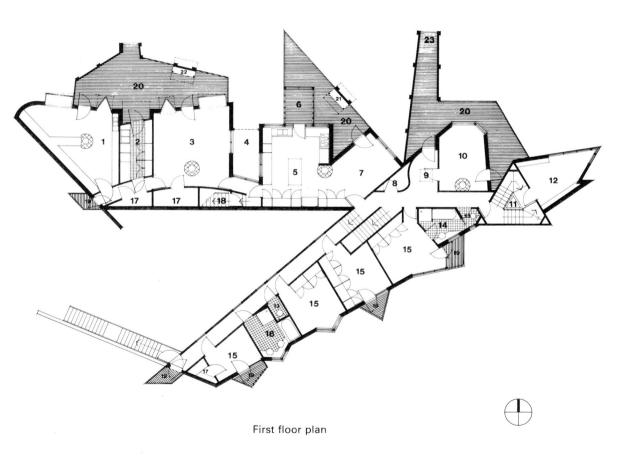

First floor plan

Entrance side

Back staircase